Conversations with
Walter Lippmann

Books by Walter Lippmann

A PREFACE TO POLITICS
DRIFT AND MASTERY
THE STAKES OF DIPLOMACY
THE POLITICAL SCENE
LIBERTY AND THE NEWS
PUBLIC OPINION
THE PHANTOM PUBLIC
MEN OF DESTINY
AMERICAN INQUISITORS
A PREFACE TO MORALS
INTERPRETATIONS 1931–1932
INTERPRETATIONS 1933–1935
THE METHOD OF FREEDOM
THE NEW IMPERATIVE
THE GOOD SOCIETY
U.S. FOREIGN POLICY: SHIELD OF THE REPUBLIC
U.S. WAR AIMS
THE COLD WAR: A STUDY IN U.S. FOREIGN POLICY
ISOLATION AND ALLIANCES: AN AMERICAN SPEAKS
TO THE BRITISH
THE PUBLIC PHILOSOPHY
THE COMMUNIST WORLD AND OURS
THE COMING TESTS WITH RUSSIA
WESTERN UNITY AND THE COMMON MARKET
CONVERSATIONS WITH WALTER LIPPMANN

With William O. Scroggs
THE UNITED STATES IN WORLD AFFAIRS 1931
THE UNITED STATES IN WORLD AFFAIRS 1932

Conversations with Walter Lippmann

TRANSCRIBED WITH THE COOPERATION OF
The Columbia Broadcasting System, Inc.

WITH AN INTRODUCTION BY
EDWARD WEEKS

An Atlantic Monthly Press Book
LITTLE, BROWN AND COMPANY · BOSTON · TORONTO

ATLANTIC–LITTLE, BROWN BOOKS
ARE PUBLISHED BY
LITTLE, BROWN AND COMPANY
IN ASSOCIATION WITH
THE ATLANTIC MONTHLY PRESS

Published simultaneously in Canada
by Little, Brown & Company (Canada) Limited

PRINTED IN THE UNITED STATES OF AMERICA

To Fred W. Friendly
The only begetter, who conceived and produced all this.
W. L.

Introduction

For nearly three and a half decades Walter Lippmann has been writing his syndicated column *Today
and Tomorrow,* in which he analyzes our foreign and
domestic policies and the character of those who are
shaping our future. It has been a unique performance, carried by some 270 newspapers here and
abroad, and of ever widening influence. A cartoon by
Barlow in the *New Yorker* of the 1930's showed two
dowagers riding in a Pullman dining car, one of
them from behind a copy of the New York *Herald
Tribune* remarking: "Of course only coffee in the
morning — a cup of coffee and Walter Lippmann is
all I need." Later, when the world was being threatened by Hitler, the *New Yorker* carried a second
drawing, this of a Thurber man and woman, with
the exclamation: "Lippmann scares me this morning."

What is remarkable about Mr. Lippmann's writing
is that it has grown stronger with the years. Not only
is he the dean of American journalists; he is the most

vigorous and most trusted opinion maker in the corps, a temperature gauge by which many Americans measure the seriousness of what is happening. Twice a week he continues to write the 1200 or more words for his column; twice a year he goes abroad to visit, to talk to, and to heed the men responsible in government. And from June to September he walks the beaches and the uplands of Mount Desert in Maine in reflection.

On the occasion of Mr. Lippmann's seventieth birthday, September 23, 1959, his fellow journalists in Washington tendered him a luncheon at the National Press Club, and in response to the toast Mr. Lippmann defined the responsibilities of a Washington correspondent in words to be remembered. "Last summer," he said, "while walking in the woods and on the mountains where I live I found myself daydreaming about how I would answer, about how I would explain and justify, the business of being opinionated and of airing opinions regularly several times a week.

"Is it not absurd, I heard the critics saying, that anyone should think he knows enough to write so much about so many things? You write about foreign policy. Do you see the cables which pour into the State Department every day from all parts of the world? Do you attend the staff meetings of the Secretary of State and his advisers? Are you a member of the National Security Council, and what about all those other countries which you write about? Do you have the run of 10 Downing Street, and how do you listen in on the deliberations of the Presidium in the Kremlin? Why don't you admit that you are an outsider and that you are therefore by definition an ignoramus? How then do you presume to interpret, much less to criticize and to disagree with, the policy of your own government, and for that matter of any other government? . . ."

And he closed with words so honest and so searching that they brought a rising acclaim: "If the country is to be governed with the consent of the governed, then the governed must arrive at opinions about what their governors want them to consent to. How do they do this?

"They do it by hearing on the radio and reading in the newspapers what the corps of correspondents tell them is going on in Washington and in the country at large, and in the world. Here we perform an essential service. In some field of interest we make it our business to find out what is going on under the surface and beyond the horizon, to infer, to deduce, to imagine and to guess, what is going on inside, and what this meant yesterday, and what it could mean tomorrow. In this we do what every sovereign citizen is supposed to do, but has not the time or the interest to do for himself. This is our job. It is no mean calling, and we have a right to be proud of it, and to be glad that it is our work."

Not long after this Fred W. Friendly, then Executive Producer of CBS Reports, now President of CBS News, had the happy idea of an hour-long interview with Mr. Lippmann, an unrehearsed Conversation conducted in Mr. Lippmann's library or in his summer place at Southwest Harbor, in which Americans would have the opportunity of watching on their television screens an extremely intelligent man dealing with extremely worrisome matters, the questions being put to him by an experienced commentator such as Howard K. Smith. These Conversations have come to be an annual event on the CBS Television Network, and the fun of the thing is to see the way Mr. Lippmann's eyes light up as he faces an unpremeditated question, and the directness, the humor, or the warning with which he seeks to illuminate his answer. "My God, my syntax" was his comment when he reread my lightly edited version of his scripts, but actually I think it is very clear when one considers the swiftness with which he has marshaled his ideas in answer to such skillful probing.

Mr. Lippmann never backs away from a hard question, and to one who reads or listens carefully, it is remarkable how farsighted his answers can be. He foresaw the necessity of Khrushchev's imposing some restraint upon the East Berliners; he foresaw the necessity "reasonably soon" for K's retirement, and although he was wrong in dismissing Goldwater as a candidate he was right in his forecast of what that nomination would cost the Republican party if it came. Throughout these seven Conversations he reverts, and always with fresh emphasis, to the major issues of our time, the great imponderables that permit no quick solution: the reunification of Germany, the question of coexistence, the threat of Red China, the extent to which Europe in her recovery will need our aid. Five correspondents — Eric Sevareid having been in charge of the last two — have taken their turn as interlocutor, and in each case the performance owes much to the forethought and friendliness with which they have conducted the discourse.

EDWARD WEEKS

Table of Contents

I

Lippmann and Howard K. Smith

What Mr. Lippmann had uppermost in his mind as he faced his first broadcast was the coming election, and what would be demanded of the man who would succeed President Eisenhower. Mr. Lippmann's view of the Cold War had been clarified by his first visit to the Soviet Union in the spring of 1958, when he had talked at length with Premier Khrushchev, and by Khrushchev's behavior and utterances in the course of his thirteen-day visit to America in September, 1959. In December, 1959, President Eisenhower embarked on a goodwill tour of some 22,000 miles which was to carry him to Europe, Asia, and Africa, and as a counterstroke within the Communist orbit, Anastas Mikoyan signed an agreement with Premier Castro for the Soviet purchase of Castro's sugar, and Khrushchev extended to President Sukarno the first of a series of credits to Indonesia. In May, 1960, John F. Kennedy defeated Hubert Humphrey in the West Virginia primary, a forecast of the victory to come, and that same month a U-2 jet reconnaissance plane piloted by Francis Gary Powers was shot down over the U.S.S.R., an act which was to result in the breaking up of a Summit Conference in Paris attended by Eisenhower, Macmillan, de Gaulle, and Khrushchev.

SMITH: Mr. Lippmann, I gathered from reading your columns in the year 1952 that you then thought that the formation of an Eisenhower administration was an urgent necessity for the nation, and I gather from reading your columns now that you're highly critical of that administration. Could you tell me why you felt that way then and why you feel the way you do now?

LIPPMANN: Well, as a matter of fact, I began to feel in 1948 that it was very necessary to the working of our political system that the Republican party should come into power and assume responsibility. They had been out of office, in 1948, for four terms; that's a very bad thing for a political party. They were becoming irresponsible; they were becoming frustrated; they were following demagogues like McCarthy. And in 1948, I was for Dewey. I thought that was the time to make a change. I thought that it was possible that we wanted a change to a Republican who was competent and who was not an isolationist, and Dewey filled that bill. Well, he failed. So by '52, it was much worse and much more urgent, and Eisenhower appeared as a possibility, and a national hero — and that had other advantages. It not only virtually insured that the Republicans would come back to power, as you might say, respectably — not on a general repudiation of everything that had gone before, and during the war, and all that — but also because Eisenhower, due to his position as a national hero, was, in my view, bound to attract McCarthy and destroy him. And that is, as a matter of fact, what happened. McCarthy soon turned from the Democrats, whom he'd been accusing of twenty years of treason, to the Republicans. And when he did that, the Republican Party dealt with him. The other thing about Eisenhower was that he alone, I thought, or rather a Republican alone, and Eisenhower as a Republican, was able to put an end to the Korean War. And the combination of those things made me feel, in '52, that it was essential to elect him, much as I admired Stevenson.

SMITH: Well, what about now?

LIPPMANN: I think that President Eisenhower is not aware of the nature of the world as it is after the two world wars, and he's out of date, and he's pursuing a policy — which I could go into in much more detail, if you wanted to — a policy which is not preparing the country for the needs of the 1960's and one which is not, in my view, meeting the real challenge of the Soviet Union.

SMITH: Do you think that failing is due to the President himself, and his unique background and training as a military man, or to the conservative advisers whom he has leaned upon? Or is it perhaps the mood of the nation? Is there a mood of complacency that he parallels?

LIPPMANN: There is a mood of complacency, of course. But I feel that his views on a number of basic principles of government no longer fit the world we live in. I'll give you a concrete example. Then, if you want to go on, we can go on with it. In his first budget, which is 1954, really, he laid it down as a principle that it was the purpose of the Federal Government, his administration in the Federal Government, to reduce the share of the national wealth that went into public purposes. This at a time when the population of the country was growing; the character of the country was changing, in that we were becoming more and more urbanized; the challenge of the Soviet Union was becoming more and more severe; and the wealth of the country was increasing.

SMITH: Well, Mr. Lippmann, in a column you wrote in September of last year when Khrushchev was here, you say that the Soviet Union is a nation with a great sense of purpose, and that we do not, at present, have that sense of purpose. And you say that without a revival of American purpose, Mr. K. is likely to win the competitive race in which he is the challenger. If he does win that race, our influence as a world power will inevitably decline. Could you expand on that?

LIPPMANN: If I remember the figures correctly, the gross national product of the Soviet economy is growing at about twelve billion dollars a year. Ours is growing, with our somewhat slower rate of growth, probably at about fifteen billion.

SMITH: Theirs twelve — ours about fifteen?

LIPPMANN: About that, yes. Now, of this increase, they direct to national purposes a much larger percentage than we direct. By national purposes I mean military purposes, education, the development of their cities, housing and planning of cities, the development of their natural resources which cannot be done by private — in any country by private — sources, like building dams and deepening channels of rivers and all that. My recollection is that their gross national product is about one-half the size of the American — but of the half, they spend about a half.

SMITH: I see. Almost fifty per cent, then, to our twenty per cent.

LIPPMANN: Yes, I may be wrong but that's my impression. The result is that their national power is growing more rapidly than ours. But the Republican

Party, under Eisenhower's leadership, does not understand the necessity of greater allocation of our resources, in a growing economy, to public needs. Therefore, he's taking risks with our defense. I don't say we're in mortal danger, but he's taking risks which I don't think we ought to take, considering how rich we are. And he is not doing the necessary things for education, and so on, which cannot be postponed any longer.

SMITH: Well, now, you've talked about allocating more resources to community and public needs, and this means finding the money to do it with, and when you talk about that, the objection is raised that this is big government or creeping socialism. What is your comment on that?

LIPPMANN: The best way to answer that is to look at what it means quantitatively. I think that the Rockefeller Report, which is the latest authoritative and impartial thing that we have, estimates that all branches of government — Federal, state, local — took about twenty per cent of our gross national product.

SMITH: So we devote about twenty per cent of our whole income.

LIPPMANN: Yes — of all the wealth produced in the United States. Now, if you take all the things that we think ought to be done, in what we call the public sector, by public spending, it would take about twenty-four per cent. You do not revolutionize an economy by rising from twenty per cent to twenty-four per cent. As for this thing about big government — that should not be confused with government. I mean, we have an inflated bureaucracy, and anything that can be done to deflate it and reduce it, well and good. But that doesn't mean you should deflate its purposes. It's really quite thoughtless of people who'd say, Let's have private economy — everybody buy an automobile. That's fine. But spend the money to produce the streets in which the automobile can run and park? That's terrible. That's government spending. That's socialism. Well, of course, they haven't really thought it through.

SMITH: Now, allocating funds for these things is another way of saying we've got to get more money to devote to community purposes.

LIPPMANN: Yes.

SMITH: How do governments get more money to devote to these purposes?

LIPPMANN: By taxation.

SMITH: Are there politicians with enough courage to ask for higher taxes?

LIPPMANN: They're just going to have to be courageous enough, because it's necessary. Before we raise the tax rate, we close what are known as some

of the loopholes in the present tax structure. It is rid-
dled with loopholes.

SMITH: Yes?

LIPPMANN: And if they were closed — I mean
even partially — the revenues to the government
would be there — I don't know what percentage of
what we need to spend, but a very considerable part
of it. And our present tax rates are based on what?
On a tax reduction made by President Eisenhower
and Mr. Humphrey in the 1954 revenue bill. Well,
there's nothing in the Constitution, or the Bible, or
anything else, which says that the tax rates of 1954
must never be changed. We've lived under higher
taxes. Now, how the tax burden should be distrib-
uted — whether it should all be on the rich or on
the poor or where — that's another question. In my
view, the merely graduated income tax is probably
not the best way to accomplish what we want to accomplish.

SMITH: Then what is the best way, do you think?

LIPPMANN: Well, it's probably to distribute it so
that consumption comes down somewhat; or rather,
as a matter of fact, it's not a question of reducing
consumption — it's of not increasing it more rapidly.

SMITH: Do you mean a sales tax on things that
might be luxury goods?

LIPPMANN: Yes. I think a sales tax or excise taxes

on sales of the things that we'd like to divert — more
to the building industry for schools and away from
unnecessarily handsome skyscrapers along Park Avenue, in New York. The way to do that is by using
taxation.

SMITH: Well, is it possible to meet part of the bill
by changing some of the expenditures we now make?
For example, we're spending a huge amount on the
farm program, which isn't working; on veterans who
have never been injured in the service of their country, and so on.

LIPPMANN: But that, I think, takes more courage
than —

SMITH: Than raising taxes.

LIPPMANN: Than raising taxes. And I've seen the
argument made that — well, why don't we reduce
these first and then go in for the public needs? And I
say the public needs can't wait.

SMITH: Yes.

LIPPMANN: We ought to do these other things.
But if we can't do them, then we'll just have to waste
the money that we waste, on the farm program and
on the veterans, and so on.

SMITH: Well, what are our public needs? What
are some of these urgent things that cannot wait?

LIPPMANN: First of all, there is the national defense. It is absolutely necessary to the peace of the

world that there should be no question at all that the American military arm is basically invulnerable. I don't mean that we can win everywhere, or that we could defeat the Russians even, but that we cannot be knocked out. The second public need, and which is urgent, is education. We are not considering the rate of growth of the school population. We are not keeping up with it. We're falling behind. And once you've failed to educate a child, you've failed, and you can't make that up later. So you have to do it currently. And it's very urgent. Because if you don't educate these children adequately, they will become the parents of children who in turn will be less adequately educated. It's a thing that degenerates if you don't deal with it promptly. We are committed, as a nation, and rightly so, to something that's never really been attempted before in the Western world — the mass education of a whole people. For instance, in Great Britain or France everybody goes to school, but only a very small percentage goes to the university. We have got the idea that everybody should be able to get to college. Now, this quantitative thing — this quantitative goal, which I'm in favor of, of course, must not be bought at the expense of quality.

SMITH: And you think we've tended to do that?

LIPPMANN: We have tended to do that, and that is our problem — to combine mass education with education for excellence. And that means — that makes education very expensive, but it's worth the price. And if we do that, we will have achieved, really more than any other, our real spiritual ideal in this country.

Then, we don't spend enough on scientific research. We spend a good deal of money on research to make certain kinds of products — commercial products, which I don't think should be counted in the basic research, because they do not really advance knowledge and they are not directed to the things that are really necessary. I mean a new cosmetic may be desirable but not necessary, and the money spent by all the chemists working on that is a diversion from the kind of thing that we ought to have — medical research and research into space things and so on.

Then, we've got to do something about the decline of our cities.

SMITH: Yes.

LIPPMANN: We are a nation which has become overwhelmingly urban in the last generation. We live in cities now. Over a hundred million Americans or more live in cities — big cities. The more you live in the city the more money you have to spend publicly. I mean, it's all very well — you can say a farmer — if you have a farmer's view — a small family farm —

does not need paved streets or public sewers — not even a public water supply. But the minute you begin to live in cities, you have to spend money publicly.

SMITH: Well, what about the ability of the Congress to face issues? I remember last year Senator Lyndon Johnson made a "State of the Union" message, in which he said the Senate would take over leadership of the nation, and then the Senate proceeded to follow the President.

LIPPMANN: In our system of government the only leadership that's possible is from the White House. The few occasions in our history when Congress, itself, has tried to lead — for instance, after the Civil War, when Congress was supreme and the President was very weak, have been periods of very bad government in this country. Another bad period was after the First World War — during the Harding period, when Congress was in the saddle. That's no good. The country can only be led, under the way our government is constructed, from the White House.

SMITH: What about the Presidency as an office? Is it a possible job, or must there be changes in it, so that one man can handle it?

LIPPMANN: The Presidency, of course, has grown into a great department of government, from being merely a personal administration, that is true, and a great many things could be done to make the burden of the job more manageable. But essentially, there's nothing, no way I can think of, that you can avoid the burden of it. That's the kind of government we have and none of us wants to change it radically. And there we are.

SMITH: Well, what do you think about our decision-making process? Is it working?

LIPPMANN: It isn't working but it could work. I think it's worse than it needs to be, if I may say so, because of President Eisenhower's training, as a staff officer in the army, which makes him avoid decisions. He wants his subordinate staff officers, his department heads, to come to him with agreed decisions. Whereas, I think, that isn't workable in civilian government — though it might work in the army.

SMITH: What's the alternative?

LIPPMANN: The alternative is for the President to decide those things. It means spending a lot more time in Washington and a lot more time listening to essentials. The next President will conduct the office very differently from President Eisenhower — no matter whether he's a Republican or a Democrat. It can't be conducted this way, through the sixties; the problems are too severe and too urgent.

SMITH: Well now, Mr. Lippmann, you've talked about the things we have to do. We have to mobilize public opinion behind these things. We have to make the right decisions at the right time. Can a loose democracy compete with a taut, centralized dictatorship in doing these things? Is democracy out of date in facing these problems?

LIPPMANN: No, I don't think so. But it does require very good leadership. I am not a pessimist about this problem, although I've written quite a lot about the faults of democracy. The thing to remember is that we're at the beginning of a new political generation. The old gentlemen, who have run the world during the war and after it, are going to retire from the stage — all of them — and the men who are going to rule, not only in this country but in the other Western democracies, are men in their forties or early fifties.

SMITH: Well, in talking about the problems we have to face, almost everything you've said has indicated that the answers are traceable back to leadership. What qualities does a leader — a President — have to have?

LIPPMANN: Well, the first thing he must have is the ability to see what matters in the excitement of daily events. He must be able to see through the latest headline to what is permanent and enduring. This ability — this second sight — is, to my mind, the quality of great leaders. Churchill has it. He's the greatest man of this century, in my view, and one of the great figures in Western history. I have unbounded admiration for that man. He has all the qualities that very great leaders have, which I call second sight, in decision and articulateness. De Gaulle has it. I put him just second to Churchill among the great men of this century — greatest in quality. And I've felt that since June, 1940, when I first read the speech he made when he landed in England, barehanded. And when you think that out of that he rallied France, and what he's made of her now, it is an absolutely fabulous performance. Theodore Roosevelt, who was my boyhood hero, had second sight. Roosevelt saw in 1900 that we were a great power — didn't wait till 1940 and Hitler to learn that.

That ability to see which way the thing is going is the basis of great leadership. The President cannot, himself, act on everything. He has to decide. So his mind has to be judicial. The function of the Presidency is to hear the arguments of the contending factions and make a decision. And that requires not only decisiveness, as everybody says, but the ability to be judicial about it. Then, of course, he must be articulate. He must be able to talk in language which not the lowest common denominator understand, but the best — what you must lead in a country are the best of the country and they will carry it on down. There's no use of the President trying to talk down to a fellow who can just about read and write. Let somebody else do that. He must talk to the people who teach the man to read and write. And for that, he requires — well, as I said, articulateness. Then, he must have sympathy; he must have the ability to feel for people who are in trouble, not only here but in Korea or in Turkey or Cuba or wherever.

SMITH: What about the practical training of Presidential candidates? Do senators make good candidates for the Presidency?

LIPPMANN: If they do, it's rather the exception. Our experience shows that on the whole, in the last hundred years or seventy-five years, the best — the most successful Presidents have been governors of big states first. That seems to be the training where you have the whole problem of a legislature and an electorate, and so on, in miniature — and it trains people. It's interesting to me — the three great Presidents of the twentieth century — I don't think there's any doubt — have been Theodore Roosevelt, Woodrow Wilson and Franklin Roosevelt.

SMITH: All governors.

LIPPMANN: All governors. Before that, surely everybody, I think, would agree that the greatest President, after Lincoln — between the death of Lincoln and 1900 — was Grover Cleveland. He'd also been a governor. Now, I don't mean — not an absolute rule. I wouldn't say that. But even being a Cabinet officer is not an adequate training.

SMITH: Well, Herbert Hoover served an apprenticeship as a Cabinet officer. What kind of a President do you think he made?

LIPPMANN: I think Hoover was a man whose instincts were better than his theories. He was an extremely sympathetic, kind, knowing man, but he had a lot of outworn theories. He'd no longer realized what the world had become, in 1929, when the roof fell in on him. And I think there's a good deal of a tragedy in that.

SMITH: Now, you mentioned Hoover's successor, Franklin D. Roosevelt, as one of the three great Presidents of the twentieth century. Could you expand on your estimate of him?

LIPPMANN: Well, I have long had mixed and confused feelings about him, having known him, as a very young man — years before he had his polio — in the First World War, when I thought he was extremely attractive. He was one of the most handsome, attractive young men — quite superficial, rather uneducated, but so charming that everybody liked him, though nobody ever conceived of him as President of the United States. Then came his illness and during that period he grew up. Even then, he had really not become the Roosevelt that the world knows. Even when he was nominated — even during the campaign of 1932, none of the New Deal was visible. That was all improvised after his election. Then, I had an in-and-out feeling about the New Deal. The first part of it I thought was very bad — the part that terminated in the attempt to pack the Supreme Court. And the second part of it, which had to do with the compensated economy, you know, the economy of balancing the business, I thought was very good. Then he became a war President, and on the whole, he was a great war President.

SMITH: What about our first postwar President — Harry Truman?

LIPPMANN: I was not a supporter of Truman at any time. I was against him in '48 and — when he was re-elected. And while I recognize that some very good things happened under Truman, also some bad things happened under him — I never thought that his quick way of shooting from the hip was the way the Presidency should be conducted. So I can't count myself an admirer of Truman.

SMITH: Could you tell me a good thing, and a bad thing?

LIPPMANN: Well, of course, under Truman the Marshall Plan was adopted. And that is probably the greatest single act of constructive statesmanship since the war. Also, NATO was founded. Those two things I'd rate very high. About the Korean War, my feelings are these: I think he was right to intervene and resist when he did. But I've never been satisfied that it was right to resist except by air and sea, which is what MacArthur and Eisenhower originally wanted to do. Even if you assume that that was all right — to fight a land war in Korea with American troops — he made a fatal mistake when, having won that war and driven the North Koreans across the Thirty-eighth Parallel, he didn't stop there and instead went on up to the Chinese border, which brought the Chinese into the war, and created a war between China and the United States which we have never been able to solve.

SMITH: Who's to blame for that — the President or his general — General MacArthur?

LIPPMANN: I blame it on the President and his Secretary of State because they are responsible — and generals don't make policy of that kind, in any well-ordered government.

SMITH: Well, that general tried to, didn't he?

LIPPMANN: I think that they were very willing in Washington. My impression is that the President and his Secretary of State were just as eager to do it.

Of course, I didn't see General MacArthur but I did know what they were doing.

SMITH: Well, how would you assess Truman's decision to use the atomic bomb against Japan?

LIPPMANN: Japan was ready for surrender before we dropped the bombs. And in my view, we should have negotiated a surrender before we dropped them. One of the things I look back on with the greatest regret, as an American, is that we were the ones that first dropped atomic bombs.

SMITH: I wonder if we could turn our thoughts abroad for a moment. Let me ask you something about the Cold War. Do you see any way out of this situation in which we and our adversaries spend huge quantities of treasure on arms which are becoming deadlier all the time, and even by accident could destroy us?

LIPPMANN: If you mean by Cold War a thing which is on the verge of a real war — a shooting war — then I think the prospects are not bad. In fact, I think they're pretty good. There's a great change in Russia, and I don't mean by that, that the Russians agree with us. What I mean is that the Russians have become concentrated on an objective which is incompatible with war, namely, the development of the

Soviet territory, which is one-sixth of the globe and is an enormously rich thing to develop, and that has become their great purpose. And they cannot improve their standard of life, they cannot succeed in any of the practical purposes that they have today, unless they can avoid war. I mean, there are countries that believe — maybe the Russians were in that position twenty-five years ago — that they could expand their system, all over the world, by conquest. But now the risks of war are enormously greater than any possible gain from it. So I believe the Russians, when they say they don't want a war.

SMITH: It seems to me that all the basic problems between us and the Russians are such hard-rock problems, I can't imagine any one giving on them. For example, in disarmament, they can't agree to it with inspection, and we can't agree without inspection, and with inspection they would have to change their whole way of life. And we cannot agree to the unification of Germany, except on our terms, which involve free elections. How can there be, then, a diplomatic expression of this improvement?

LIPPMANN: Leaving out us for the moment, I think the agreement between Western Europe and the Soviet Union about the future of Germany is much greater than appears on the surface. Where they agree is that neither the Russians nor the

French nor the British want reunified Germany. Nobody will say this because it would be political dynamite for Dr. Adenauer in Germany to admit it. But the fact is that all British and French planning is based on the theory that Germany is not going to be reunited. So is the Soviet planning. Well, when you've agreed on as big a point as that, you've gone an awful long way toward a relaxation of tension, even if you're still disagreed about Berlin.

SMITH: What about disarmament?

LIPPMANN: I belong to the old school that thinks that disarmament follows political agreement — never precedes it. As long as we were in a position, as we were ten years ago, at the zenith of Stalin, where war was a real danger, it was foolish to talk about disarmament. It would have been foolish to think of disarming, but insofar as the feeling grows that we have no vital issue to go to war about — nothing worth a war — I think you'll gradually get what I would call fringe agreements about disarmament. The most obvious one is the cessation of nuclear testing.

SMITH: But — how does this jibe with their increasing pressure on Berlin?

LIPPMANN: Well, I don't think there's an increasing pressure on Berlin. I don't think the Russians are out to absorb West Berlin into East Germany. And I think they have two reasons. One is we won't let them do it, and therefore they cannot risk a war over that issue. But there's another reason, and that is that West Berlin would be an indigestible thing in the system of East Germany. And I think they know it. Those West Berliners would be — two million and a half of them in a country of eighteen million — a very dangerous lot of people in their country. So I think what they want is not to absorb them but to insulate them from East Germany and from the West. They want to create a little community there, which is not Communist — has no position in the Communist world — on the other hand, which is not an allied outpost — has no Western troops in it — and so on.

SMITH: So they want to get rid of us, is that it?

LIPPMANN: They want to get rid of the Western presence in Berlin, and they would probably settle for some kind of arrangement. I don't say we ought to accept this. But I mean settle for some kind of arrangement with the United Nations force, guaranteeing the freedom of West Berlin.

SMITH: Well, we've talked about our Russian adversary — what about Red China? Is the time approaching when it may be wise to acknowledge the existence of that country which contains a quarter of the earth's population?

LIPPMANN: I tell you, as a matter of fact, we do recognize them — and we are actually negotiating with the Chinese, in Warsaw. Warsaw, about the relations over Formosa. The question of their coming into the UN — I think the right thing would be if they were admitted to the UN — if they will adhere to the agreement for nuclear testing, that could be taken as proof that they mean to be a peace-loving state under the definitions of the United Nations — and I would hold that out to them as the price, really.

SMITH: Well, in fact, without Chinese agreement, a nuclear test ban would not work, is that not so?

LIPPMANN: No. I don't think so because they cannot do much testing without Russian help.

SMITH: I was assuming the Russians might use some of their territory to test on.

LIPPMANN: Ah! You mean that they'll cheat? The Russian interest is, I think, not to have the Chinese have the bombs. Because who would be the most likely victim of them? We? The Chinese, even if they get a few bombs, can't do anything to us. I mean, they don't have a great delivery system and all that, which is much more expensive than the bombs. But Russia, with four thousand miles of frontier — they've got to look out for the Chinese. Now, the question of the United States having diplomatic relations with China is still another question. They'll get into the UN, I imagine, before we recognize them. And there, we have certain issues that we have to settle with them before we can establish diplomatic relations. We're at war with them — technically. . . .

SMITH: Yes.

LIPPMANN: And they're holding people of ours prisoners, and so on. Those have to be released. We have to come to settle our outstanding issues.

SMITH: Well, you've talked about our relations with our adversaries — what about our relations with our allies? Do we have a bright future for the Alliance, or does it face problems that may break it up?

LIPPMANN: In answering that question, you must distinguish between the NATO military establishment, as it now exists, and the alliance of the Atlantic community, which is a much bigger thing. In my view, the Atlantic community is a fact of history which cannot be dissolved and won't be dissolved. And we are inevitable allies in any struggle which is of vital interest to us. There is some question as to just where the boundaries of the Atlantic community are. Germany has never been part of it, for instance. We hope at least to bring West Germany into it. But broadly speaking, the Atlantic community is an indissoluble thing. It was made by God and geography and not by man.

SMITH: Well, is there anything we can do to aid God and geography to make it work better?

LIPPMANN: I think yes. I think NATO, which is the military establishment, is probably getting obsolete and should be revised. I can remember when our great fear was that the Red Army was going to start rolling through West Germany and into Paris. And that was when we started NATO — NATO was started here — that was the idea, how to stop that. Nobody thinks that any more — not in the missile age. So the thing is a little bit — tends to be obsolete. And that's what General de Gaulle is complaining about. General de Gaulle wants the NATO, and he wants the Atlantic community, and all that. But he's a far-seeing general, with a much greater military mind than anybody who's ever put his mind on NATO. And I think, when he says it needs to be revised, I'm willing to listen to him.

SMITH: What would you say is going to be the biggest single job the next President of the United States will have?

LIPPMANN: Mobilizing the country to meet the Soviet challenge. I don't use this in a military sense — but to gather together and make available to the nations our wealth, our growing wealth, for the purpose of meeting the competition of the Soviet Union and of solving our own problems. That has to be made clear to the people — that this is the big task of the 1960's. We're going to have to grow up to the times, or fall way behind in the competition.

SMITH: Well, it's become almost a recent tradition for the Legislature, in this country, to be dominated by one party, and the Administration or the Executive Branch to be run by the other party. What do you think of that arrangement? Some people have praised it.

LIPPMANN: It's a very recent thing and I think a passing one. In our history, if a President was elected, he usually carried the House with him. And if he was at all successful, he carried the Senate with him by the next mid-term election. No, I don't think the split is a good thing. I think it's a bad thing — undesirable.

SMITH: Now, in the next election, according to the opinion polls, the Congress is certain to be won by the Democrats, but a leading Democrat said to me recently: "While the Republicans can't win the coming Presidential election, the Democrats can lose it." If that happens do you think it will be a calamity that the two are divided once more?

LIPPMANN: Yes, and I think it would be worse under Mr. Nixon than it was under Mr. Eisenhower. Because President Eisenhower has a prestige which

Mr. Nixon can't hope to attain, and his relations with the Democrats, who nearly nominated him in '48, are very much better than Mr. Nixon's.

SMITH: Well now, about our immediate future, are you optimistic or pessimistic?

LIPPMANN: I don't believe in being pessimistic because what's the good of giving up before you're finished — and I don't intend to be pessimistic about it. What is more, I think we don't know what the country in the sixties will be like, with a new crop of young men under good leadership. Today we're at the end of something that is petering out and aging and about finished. And I think the country survived a period, in my experience, after World War I, which is very like what we've been through in the last few years. That was the great Jazz Age of the 1920's — and you wouldn't have supposed people would ever have a serious thought again. But that wasn't true — and it will pass as soon as the country gets purposes which are articulated by an effective leader.

SMITH: Now, in regard to the U–2, what was our basic mistake? What did we do that was wrong?

LIPPMANN: The fundamental error we made — leaving out the very sizable error of having the flight at that time, right before the Summit — leaving that out, the fundamental error we made was that we didn't play the game of espionage as all the world has played it for centuries. And the game of espionage requires — it is part of the rules of the game understood in every country — that if your spy is caught, you disown him. You never do anything for him. You don't admit even if you ever heard of him. Now, we were in a very difficult position because they had caught not only the spy but his plane and the camera, and everything else.

SMITH: And a lot of paraphernalia.

LIPPMANN: A lot of paraphernalia — and all that. But still, we talked too much. The thing to do was to have said practically nothing, and said, on this incident, we'll have to investigate it some more — and it's very unfortunate, and we're not quite clear just what happened. And that's all you do say. And everybody knows you're not really telling the truth. But that is what the rules are. Now, I think to understand that, you have to realize that every country does spying, in one form or another, and they do this spying with the best thing they can find to do it with. If they happen to have a good plane, they'll use that; if not, they all expect — don't want to be put in the position where if they catch a spy, they have to make a war about it — because they do it themselves. So that's why the game has developed — and we didn't play that game. I think that was our great mistake.

SMITH: I think many people would think you hit on the key failing of the American people. We talked too much. [Laughter]

LIPPMANN: We talk too much, yes.

SMITH: May I ask you — is it possible that if Eisenhower had four more years instead of six months, Khrushchev would not have hit him as hard, but he felt safe in planning to deal with a new President now, so he made the most of it?

LIPPMANN: I thought he lost his temper. I think there was every evidence that he lost his temper. He had built up Eisenhower, in Russia, as his great friend, and as the man of peace — and here was the same man who, for four years, had been flying over Russian territory — Khrushchev was violently angry, disappointed, and also under attack from his critics.

SMITH: Now, what about the theory I have heard from some people that after the President's big, jubilant receptions in India, and the receptions he could expect in the Far East, Khrushchev was afraid that it would become a political phenomenon if the President arrived in Russia and was equally jubilantly received — and he felt he had to stop that?

LIPPMANN: Yes, but the thing is the President had his triumphal tour in the autumn, in India, so Khrushchev knew all about that, and he had all winter in which to consider, and then he went right on setting a date for the conference, and even going to Paris. So I can't believe that he was really afraid of the crowds. In fact, they were drumming up crowds for the President.

SMITH: Since we last talked, the world has seemed to come apart at the seams. The U–2 affair has happened; the Summit Conference has collapsed, and the Japanese crisis involving our treaty with Japan has happened. I would like to ask you to try to assess the meaning of these events. How big are they? A Gallup poll recently suggested that most people now think war with Russia is likely. Do you think that these events have been important and durable, or are they things that can be corrected relatively easily?

LIPPMANN: No, I don't think the world's come apart and I don't think that the war is more likely than it was before. But, on the other hand, the events that have happened will have a great effect on the American position, particularly in Asia. And those events — I think we're only at the beginning of the chain of events that have been set in motion by the U–2 incident — by the discovery that these bases —

American bases — around the outer rim of Asia
were being used for purposes which the Soviet Union
resented, and was threatening to retaliate about.
We've only begun to see the consequences of that.
There's nothing in the world that could protect Japan
or Formosa, or any of these countries right on the
edge. The only thing that can protect them is the fact
that we would retaliate, but in the process they
wouldn't be in very happy condition. I expect to see a
growth of neutralism in a more and more insistent
and even violent form, such as we've already begun
to see in Japan, spread all around that semicircle
which extends from Japan through Korea, Formosa,
Vietnam to Pakistan and Turkey.

SMITH: Well now, there's an appearance at least,
of increased unity in Western Europe, among our allies, as a result of these troubles. Can it be that the
case of Japan was just an isolated incident?

LIPPMANN: I think Europe is different from Asia,
and I think in Europe the violence of Khrushchev's
language — the fact that he broke off the Summit
Meeting — caused a rallying of sentiment to the
United States — a rally that probably would not have
taken place if Khrushchev had not behaved so badly.
But in Asia the situation is different. In these countries, where the bases are around the outer edge of
the Soviet Union, and of China — there the people

feel themselves threatened, in a way they never felt before.

SMITH: Well now, in regard to our alliances, there is at present in Washington a strong mood of reappraisal. Could you suggest what general lines such a reappraisal might follow?

LIPPMANN: I think you might say, speaking broadly, that there are two lines it will have to follow. One is the line of devising weapons that do not require bases in weak countries, right near the Soviet Union. That is a job for the Pentagon. It's a question of being able to get along without the bases. We've already made up our minds to get along without the bases in Morocco, in Iceland, and sooner or later we're going to have to get out of the bases that are in positions where the country is incapable of defending itself in case there's retaliation from the Soviet Union. That means longer ranges, missiles, all that is a technical matter. But I think it's true to say the Pentagon is already working on the plans for that kind of military armament. The other line is that we have to find a way, through diplomacy, of gradually converting the policy of lining up these countries as military allies, to improving the position of neutrality for those countries. To illustrate the point — for a long time we had really bad relations with India, because we were always trying to line up India in a military sense, and the Indians wouldn't join. When we gave up that policy and accepted the neutralism of India, we became quite popular in India. That was helped, to be sure, by the Chinese aggression on the Indian frontier. But the fear of the United States diminished when we ceased to want to use them as a military base.

SMITH: Now, the stock fear that is expressed in Washington is, Japan will go neutralist, and then eventually it will be on the slippery slope and will go over to the other side.

LIPPMANN: I know that is being said. But I think it's not a sound argument. I think that the presence of foreign troops or airplanes and military establishments tends to provoke — to promote Communist propaganda in the country. Now, people said that when Egypt was neutral it would become Communist — that hasn't happened. They said Iraq was going to go that way — it didn't. There's no evidence that the presence of American military missions and bases stops these countries from becoming Communist. I think the American position, in some respects, is too expanded. I think we've overexpanded, at the end of World War II. We'll draw back somewhat, especially in the Far East. But basically the country isn't going to be affected by that. Our influence, if we are able to solve our own problems and deal with our own affairs well, will expand. And the greatest influence we can have in the world comes from proving that we can make a big democracy like this work.

II

Lippmann and Howard K. Smith

The timetable leading up to this broadcast was one of many changes in the Western Hemisphere. When Premier Castro nationalized the banks and the American-owned industries in Havana, the United States retaliated by placing an embargo on all exports to Cuba except medical supplies and food. In November, 1960, John Fitzgerald Kennedy was elected President, and in January, 1961, we severed diplomatic relations with Cuba. March saw the creation of the Peace Corps and in April came the ill-fated invasion of the Bay of Pigs, resulting in the capture and death of Cuban refugees. In New Orleans two white elementary schools were the first to be desegregated in the Deep South, but this optimistic beginning was counterbalanced by the racial violence which broke out in Birmingham and Montgomery, Alabama, when freedom riders protested against the Jim Crow segregation in the buses. Abroad the Communist forces of North Vietnam invaded Laos, and in January, 1961, the French voted in favor of granting Algeria self-determination. South Africa became a republic and severed her ties with the British Commonwealth.

SMITH: In a column about a year ago you said that the first thing a good President should have is his ability to see through to what is permanent and enduring. This second sight is the quality of great leaders. Do you think that Kennedy has that second sight?

LIPPMANN: I think he's capable of having it. And perhaps when we get into this more, we'll find that he showed some weaknesses in that respect.

SMITH: Well, what has President Kennedy demonstrated so far?

LIPPMANN: What he has done in the four or five months is first to carry on in all its essentials the Eisenhower economic philosophy and the Eisenhower international commitments, and yet never explain to the country that those can be changed. It's like the Eisenhower administration thirty years younger. That's the way he started, but in the meantime, that isn't the way he's going to go. He's been — not moving in a new direction, but changing the direction in which he's going to move. Now I think that in the next year he will make the great decision, whether he can afford to balance the budget in the

Eisenhower sense and allow the economy to remain at a fairly quiet level, or whether he wants to give it a real push upward by tax reduction and measures like that. That's going to be decided in the coming months. And a weakness of President Kennedy's is that he has never explained these things to the American people.

SMITH: Now, Mr. Nixon has said that, Senator Fulbright has said that, and you have said that. Yet he's one of our most articulate — he's spoken more than Mr. Eisenhower did.

LIPPMANN: I know — but he hasn't explained. He has not explained what his economic challenge is, and what it's going to require in the way of much stronger measures in regard to tax reduction — probably government spending and credit action. He never explained why, if he wants to do all these things such as fight the Cold War and win it, really outdo the Communists, it's got to be done at full blast to the American economy, with a production of fifty billions more than we produced this year. He needs that money to do it! That's never been explained to our people, so they have no sense of urgency. And he has never explained to them the very unpleasant fact which he didn't create — it's not his fault — that we have moral commitments and legal commitments around — mainly around the rim of Asia, which were built up before he took office and when we were the supreme military power in the world. And coming down from being supreme to being only equal is an awful wrench for every country, and it makes people frustrated and angry and they don't think it ought to be true, and so on, and it's a hard thing to swallow, but that's what he's going to have to do.

SMITH: Can you understand why he has not communicated? He's an extremely articulate President. He seems to know the value of television. He's made a great many speeches. Yet he doesn't seem to have got his case across and there's a great deal of confusion in America as to what we're about.

LIPPMANN: Well, I put it to this — that he's a very quick and intelligent man himself. Reads very fast, understands very fast; and it bores him to explain things. He hasn't got the patience. He ought to have the patience that a teacher must have, who is willing to start where the pupil or the hearer is, and explain it step by step as he goes along — Kennedy tells them what it is at the end, and he likes to make decisions and announce them, but he doesn't explain them.

SMITH: Mr. Lippmann, I'd like to ask you something that I think is basic. Is it possible that a free, loose-jointed, easy-going society like the American democracy can compete with a tightly concentrated, tightly controlled, secret dictatorship like that of the Soviet Union and Red China?

LIPPMANN: That is the drama of our age. That's the question, and that is why many of us think that the Kennedy administration has to get going and moving rapidly or we won't be able to do it. I wouldn't like for a moment to underestimate how formidable this competition is, and this threat. It's very formidable, and when you see people running around this country and wanting to abolish the income tax and turn the Federal Government back into a Confederation of States, you despair of the possibility of persuading them to do what we're going to have to do, and that what we're going to have to do will take a lot of money, and a very strong government.

SMITH: Well, if Mr. Kennedy set himself one main goal in the election campaign, it was to resurrect America's fallen prestige. Do you think that in his legislative program he is doing the right things necessary to that end?

LIPPMANN: He's — I don't believe he's really got started doing that, because he is not sure of himself. Because he's conscious of his small majority, because he's conscious that he hasn't got a really effective working majority in Congress for important measures, and because I take it that he judges that the mood of the country is not in favor of doing the things which would really create a new sense of prestige. Because in the last analysis, American prestige depends not on arms, although we must have arms. It depends on the example we set to the world, and if we set the example of a very brilliantly active economy and society in which we were dealing with all our problems actively, our prestige would rise in the world.

SMITH: In the President's speech the other night, the only thing that he appealed to the American people about was to give support to his program for foreign aid. Now, judging from the mood on Capitol Hill, this is not a good year for foreign aid. Lots of previous supporters are criticizing it, and this is the year in which Laos, which we heavily aided, has gone over to the adversary, and in which South Korea, which we aided even more heavily, has abandoned democracy. Is there a good case in favor of foreign aid that isn't being made?

LIPPMANN: I would say that the United States can no more refuse to contribute to foreign aid in the world than the richest man in town can refuse to contribute to the Community Chest. You just can't live in the world community — we couldn't live — refusing to aid anybody. Now the nature of the method of aiding is very debatable. And I hope and believe that there is a movement on foot to reform some of its worst abuses. It is true, as some of the liberal critics in the Congress have been saying, that a lot of this money — as in Laos, which is a peculiarly bad case of how the thing failed — a lot of this money simply enriched the upper class, who exploited, who flaunted their riches all over and increased the hatred of the poor for the rich. And that made them very fertile ground for Communist propaganda. In other places, we've undoubtedly spent much too much money on armies that have no military value whatsoever from the point of view of our interests but are kept there, are paid for, by us in order to keep them loyal to the king or ruler of the country so they won't overthrow him. Those are great abuses. On the other hand, if the world isn't going to get into that landslide into Communism which Khrushchev predicts, there have to be anchor points in all the continents which show that prosperity and a certain amount of social justice can be achieved by another way than the Communist way. And that means that you must focus your energy, your aid on key countries.

Now, if you ask me what they are — the key country in Asia is India. If India can be made to work as a successful, democratic state, the influence of that will spread all over Southeast Asia, no matter who takes over in Laos in the next few months, and all over Indonesia and all over. The key country in Latin America is not Cuba. It's Brazil. And I don't know — I would hesitate to say just which is the key country in Africa, but I imagine it might be Nigeria. And I think in those cases we ought to focus our aid, not necessarily stopping this other aid, which is really a form of bribery to keep them quiet, but focus the big stuff and do enough to do it. There's no use building half a bridge across a river — you've got to build a whole bridge.

SMITH: You've made that point about foreign aid very strongly, and what impresses me is that the President, in talking to the American people and calling on them for action, did not make it as strongly.

LIPPMANN: Well, you've just talked about the conclusion of the speech, which dealt with foreign aid. I would say that that showed some of his defects as a political leader. He talked to the American people as if they were suffering from some terrible burden in foreign aid where they are not suffering from any burden. He should have told them, considering how grim the outlook is, that that was a first installment, and a very small one, of what they're going to have to pay, and that they mustn't think that they can just cut it down and have everything just the way they like it in the world. One of the great difficulties he runs into is that in the public mind is all that talk about spending, and he doesn't want to be labeled a spender, and he's quite right. I mean, that's political poison. But you see, the public mind, it's — people will have to get over it and learn better. Let's say if a man borrows money from a bank to build a movie house, or a dance hall, that is investment. If the city spends money to build a schoolhouse, that's spending. And that's wicked. Now actually we're about the only government in the world that keeps its accounts in this way — the only government in the world that doesn't distinguish between public spending and public investment — and that has to be cleared up. I don't know how to do it, but I think —

SMITH: Well, as long as the President fears the label "spender" and doesn't explain it, won't we always remain with this?

LIPPMANN: That's true. That is undoubtedly true. And he is haunted by the thought that Eisenhower probably could have been elected this time if he'd run again, and that that's what the country believes.

SMITH: Some people see our salvation in not what we do, but what happens to the Communists. Now, Charles Bohlen, who's probably our outstanding Soviet expert in the State Department, made a speech a short while ago in which he said that if we can just hold things for another ten years, Russian Communism may lose its aggressive revolutionary momentum the way Islam did in the Middle Ages, and we may be able then to get along with it. Do you find any consolation in that thought?

LIPPMANN: Well, I think it is dangerous to find consolation in that thought. I hope that will be true, but that is a little bit like Khrushchev's inevitability doctrine in reverse, and I don't think things are inevitable. I think men have to act to make the inevitable happen.

SMITH: Now, this is the second time you've met Khrushchev in Russia, and I think you've met him here in the United States as well. Could you give us an assessment of him? Could you measure him against some American public figure?

LIPPMANN: I've been asked that by a number of people, and the only trouble is that the man who he most reminds me of is not known well enough to people today — it's too long ago — but that was Governor Alfred Smith of New York. They have these things in common: Smith had enormous instinctive sense of what every man in his constituency — New York, New York City — was thinking. Khrushchev has that. He's got antennae all over the place. He has the capacity to talk to them, as Smith had, about the most difficult subjects, the economy, and how to do it, and make them think it's funny and interesting. Al Smith used to go down to the Bowery when he was

Governor of New York, and make a speech explaining the budget of New York State, than which there couldn't be anything more uninteresting, and he'd have them in roars of laughter. Well, Khrushchev has that quality, and then he has — I think that is the key to Khrushchev, that he is a politician and he would have been a successful politician in any country. He's not like Stalin, a sort of Oriental despot who works in the back with cloak and dagger. The President and he ought to come to some common feeling, because they're both politicians.

SMITH: Well, now they've met. Do you think that these two politicians did achieve some common feeling? It's hard to detect any from what the President said on television the other day.

LIPPMANN: I think the common feeling they've achieved is a realization of the terrible danger that they both run, if their differences are allowed to bring them to the point up some dead end street where there's no choice for one or the other or both except surrender or a suicidal war. That's the common thing they've got.

SMITH: The President, in his speech to the people afterwards, said that the most somber aspect of the talks was the discussion about Germany and Berlin.

LIPPMANN: Oh well, I think there's no doubt at all that the central problem is Germany and Berlin,

and that all these other things they discussed —
Laos and nuclear testing and disarmament, and the
general movement of Communism in the uncommit-
ted lands — are all related to this central issue,
which is the focus of the Cold War. That's the focal
point where, if there's going to be a third world war,
it will come. Khrushchev said, when I talked to him,
"I would agree to a united Germany if it were Communist." He said, "But you won't agree to that —
and I won't agree to a united Germany if it has to
give up Communism and become like Adenauer's
Germany. So there's no possibility of uniting them."
In fact, on that there is a curious agreement between Khrushchev and de Gaulle, or for instance,
Khrushchev and Macmillan. We have always ad-
hered to the idea that Germany ought eventually to
be reunited. But we don't press it because we know
it's not practical. Now at the same time there are
left in Berlin, in West Berlin, two and a half million
Germans who are not Communists at all, who are
very anti-Communist, whose sympathies, whose ties,
whose economic connections, whose culture, everything, is with the West, and who are democratic
people, and we have an absolutely unquestioned
obligation of honor to see that they are not crushed,
or not enslaved, or not starved out, or anything else.

SMITH: Well, could you summarize on the basis

of your conversation with Khrushchev what he wants and what he would be willing to negotiate about regarding Berlin?

LIPPMANN: All I can tell you is that Khrushchev says he wants to negotiate. When it came to negotiation he might stall — as we know from the experience with the nuclear test ban and everything else. But I would not pass up the chance to do that, if we can negotiate with the Soviet Union a new treaty which guarantees the future of Germany — of Berlin — that specifies what roads shall always be open to it, what airports, what harbors, what canals, all that spelled out in great detail and signed by the four powers who occupy Germany, by the two Germanys — and that's one of the rubs, because that's what the West Germans don't want — but signed by the East Germans — I don't think the thing would be good unless you got their signature — and registered at the United Nations. Then, in addition to that, there will have to remain in Berlin for some time to come British, French, and American troops. Khrushchev does demand that if American and French and British troops are to stay, then Russian troops should also be there, and that they all should be there in very small amounts. I mean, they should be symbolic, which is after all, all they are anyway. And my own view is that the thing he wants more than anything

else, and I'd like to tell you why he wants it, I think
— he wants to give legal status to the East German
state. He said to me, "I know you wouldn't recognize
the East German state." That is, I mean, we wouldn't
have an ambassador from the East German state. We
wouldn't send an ambassador to it. But it would be
allowed to sign the document, which would give it a
certain recognition, and it's what's called in diplomacy de facto recognition.

SMITH: Yes. Well, if what Mr. Rusk mentioned
takes place, that is, a crisis is provoked in the summer or fall and the Russians hand over control of our
communications with Berlin to the East German
puppets, what would you be in favor of doing?

LIPPMANN: Well, as I understood Khrushchev, a
separate peace treaty is a last resort. He doesn't want
to do it. He said half a dozen times, "I don't want the
tension. I know it'll create tension. I want to avoid it.
But in the last run, I've got to do it." And I'll tell you,
if you like, later why he thinks he's got to do it.

SMITH: Could you tell me now?

LIPPMANN: Yes. I asked him — I had been asked
to ask him by an American authority whom I won't
identify, but a friend of mine. He said, "See if you
can find out whether he wouldn't at least be willing
to have a standstill — that is, leave everything where
it is for, say, five years. In five years we'll all be older

and wiser and a lot of things can happen, and we've cooled off, and maybe then we can negotiate; but it's all very difficult to negotiate now — what with the German elections and all these things." Well, I tried that on him, and I said, "Why are you in such a hurry?" And he said, "I'm in a hurry because I want the frontiers of Germany, and the status of Berlin, and the demarcation line between the two German states settled in a treaty before," and then he said, "before Hitler's generals in West Germany get the atomic bomb." And he said, "They're going to get it. They're already being trained how to use it. They haven't got the warheads, but they're going to get it, and they surely will get it in four or five years. And they'll get it from you, or they'll get it from the French, who'll be able to make them by that time. And if that comes, then the great danger for Europe exists, because either by their attacking East Germany and overrunning East Berlin — or the other way around, that the East Germans rise and they go to their defense — either way, there'll be nothing to stop it. Nobody will have any agreements. You won't intervene — and there we'll be with a very dangerous war on our hands. So we must have a treaty first. And that is what I'm pressing for. But I want to get those frontiers fixed so that if either Germany moves, in a military sense, in the next four or five years, it will be the aggressor." Now, that's his argument, and that's why he's in a hurry.

SMITH: Well, what's the next step? What do we do now?

LIPPMANN: I think the next step is one which involves a change in our basic approach to the German problem. We have taken the line, conventionally, that everything in Berlin is as good as it could be from our point of view, that any change in the situation of Berlin would be for the worse; therefore, we must stand firm and stand pat. That's Dr. Adenauer's view. Change nothing. Fight — threaten to fight — if anything is changed. Don't negotiate; it can't be negotiated. You'll only weaken it. Now the other view, which is the one I share, is that the situation in Berlin is not good — that Berlin is in a state of chronic crisis, which means on the Russian side, Soviet side, that any time that Khrushchev wants to put on a little pressure, he could just turn the screw a little bit in Berlin, and the whole world is focused on Berlin, while something's going on in Iran or Cuba or heaven knows where. That is very disadvantageous to the West.

The other thing is that I don't believe the people of Berlin, West Berlin, or of Germany believe the present situation is good, because they come back to us every few months and demand that we should again cross our hearts and swear that we will go to war for Berlin. And if they were sure of it, if they didn't think it was something that couldn't last forever, they wouldn't feel — wouldn't be doing that. I think our position should be not that any change in the guarantees of the rights of the people of Berlin is a defeat and a surrender, but that those guarantees should be improved, if it's possible to improve them. They're not very good today. We should say — we should take the position that the freedom of Berlin, in the sense of their ability to govern themselves, to live their own life, to keep their physical and economic and spiritual and political contacts with the Western world, cannot be touched. We won't negotiate about that, but the legal basis and the statutory rights that go with that are negotiable. They never were negotiated. The thing is all a blotter of catch-can — the thing is made by generals and various people, and we ought to say — I would like to see us say to Khrushchev, "We don't like Berlin the way it is. We want to improve it, and if you can negotiate with us an improvement, we'll be very interested."

SMITH: Well, people who say that you can't reach an agreement with the Russians generally cite the fate of the nuclear test ban talks in Geneva. The President sounded very pessimistic about that.

Khrushchev doesn't seem, now, to want any agreement on it. How do you explain that?

LIPPMANN: We talked quite a lot about the nuclear test, and my explanation will have to be a guess, but the fact is that he's clearly not terribly interested in it. Now, there are several possible explanations, and they may all of them be true. One is, part of the agreement would have to be that China would be included and he may not be able to deliver China. I'm inclined to think that has a good deal to do with it, because he talks about our not being able to deliver France. But I think that's his way of saying that he can't deliver China, because when he talked about France to me, he said, "Well, what's the good of an agreement if France doesn't sign it? She'll test for you. You'll just ask her to go and test them in the Sahara Desert." And I said, "And China will test for you." And he sort of looked slightly amused, because he likes to be challenged sometimes, and he said, "That's a fair question, but China isn't able to test yet." He thinks the weapons the Russians have got are really good enough. And while we seem to be very interested in developing bigger weapons that weigh less, he has these enormous rockets. I don't think that's a practical problem for him.

SMITH: Well, I'd like to talk to you now about the

latest Russian diplomatic creation, what Mr. Mikoyan called the "troika" system of control. In short,
that almost everything, nuclear test bans and the
United Nations and anything else, be controlled by
three people, one a Westerner, one a Communist
and one a neutral, and each of those has a veto.
Now, if that is applied, wouldn't that stagnate all international activity?

LIPPMANN: Yes. It's a fairly recent dogma.
Troika, you know, comes from a Russian thing where
three horses pull a cart or a sleigh, and if one horse
sits down then the two can't move. I didn't speak to
Mr. Khrushchev about this particular point, but I
did to a very close adviser of his, a Soviet official. I
said, "Why three?" He said, "Well, we really mean
two." He said, "We really mean that everything must
be done by agreement between the United States
and the U.S.S.R. We brought in the third because
they're there. They have no power, of course, but
they're there and it looks better to include them."

SMITH: Well, does this not threaten the entire
future of the United Nations?

LIPPMANN: Yes. The future of the United Nations is very much threatened by the fact that although Mr. Hammarskjold has another two years, I
think, he couldn't be re-elected at present, and no-

body else like him could be elected, and there's quite a good chance that if there is no understanding reached with the Russians on this point, which is — I wouldn't regard it as inflexible. It's negotiable, but I don't know how negotiable. There just won't be a Secretary-General, and if there's no Secretary-General, the UN will be reduced to a debating society, or the Security Council will meet, and — but it won't be able to order anything.

SMITH: In addition to Russian intransigence, there's another change in the United Nations, and that is the admission of a very great number of brand new nations, the leaders of many of which have shown themselves to be not very responsible and to be highly volatile. Isn't it dangerous for the United States to leave our fate to be decided by a body in which these people have the balance of power?

LIPPMANN: You know, Khrushchev pointed that out to me, and he said, "Now you don't want a veto, because you still think you have a majority, and you can elect the Secretary-General, and so on, and it's all favorable to you, but pretty soon you won't be able to elect a majority, and then you'll wish you had a veto. So, in the end, you're going to want just what we want."

SMITH: Well, Mr. Lippmann, we haven't talked yet about NATO. Now, in a recent column you said that the basis for our difficulties with de Gaulle is the fact that he does not believe that America can be depended upon as a protector of Western Europe.

LIPPMANN: His view is that with modern and nuclear weapons so destructive it is suicide even for the biggest country to be attacked. Therefore no country will risk being attacked for any other country. There'd always be the hope, well, I will stay out of this and let it go by me. Therefore, he says, the old idea of NATO, which was born before both sides had nuclear weapons, while we alone had them, is out of date. It cannot be depended upon. Now, the situation is such that if — which I don't think is likely at all — but if the Soviets were going to use a nuclear weapon, they would have to strike the United States first, and then they might strike other points in Europe where there are American nuclear bases. And he doesn't want France to be in the line of fire. He also wants to have France able, on its own, to be sufficiently dangerous — "too hot to handle" is really the de Gaulle policy for France. Where our hope with de Gaulle lies is in finding a way to agree with him on the fact that nothing great in the world, nothing that might involve nuclear weapons shall be done without full consultation in advance.

That's what he wants. He's afraid that we won't protect him. He is also afraid that we'll start a war in
which he'll be involved. And I'm sorry to say, or
maybe I should — anyway, it is a fact that he has
not got a high opinion of American military leadership or political leadership.

SMITH: Well now, I wonder if Mr. de Gaulle's
appraisal of American leadership is changed since
he met President Kennedy. I noticed that in one of
his toasts at a dinner he said, "I now have more confidence in your country."

LIPPMANN: I think President Kennedy made a
strong personal impression on him, as certainly General de Gaulle made on the President, and the personal relationship of those two men is better than
the personal relationship between any head of the
French Government and the American Government
has been, I would say, since before World War II.
I would say that the utmost that anyone can say,
with any reasonable certainty, is that he feels that
in President Kennedy he has a man who is capable
of understanding his military views. I think he felt,
beforehand, that he was up against a stone wall, and
wouldn't be listened to.

SMITH: The most mysterious of all the events
that have happened is the Cuban debacle. Now, how
could a decision like that go through our best mili-

tary minds, and be okayed by the chiefs of our Intelligence — be okayed by the brilliant men who
surround Kennedy in the White House and the ex-
perts in the State Department, and get past the
President himself? That's still a mystery to me.

LIPPMANN: I think the answer you come to is
that the advice to go ahead, the green light for doing
it, or the energy demanding that we go ahead, all
came from senior advisers. The junior advisers, the
new men who've come to Washington with Kennedy, were not strong enough, perhaps not wise
enough, all of them, although some may have been,
to tell the President to overrule people with such
eminence as the people who advised him to do it. I
think there he didn't feel that he knew enough to
overrule the CIA — the Chiefs of Staff, what there
was of the State Department, and so on.

SMITH: Well, I suppose when you think that
Abraham Lincoln, perhaps our greatest President,
took almost two years before he dared to fire his
general who he thought was not doing his duty, then
Kennedy's behavior is quite understandable.

LIPPMANN: I think that he's a man who can learn.
I think he's learned that more than any other thing
from Cuba.

SMITH: Just after the Cuban fiasco, President
Kennedy paid a visit to General MacArthur, and

General MacArthur is said to have told the President, "A lot of chickens are coming home to roost and you're in the chicken coop." Do you believe it's true that most of these problems were situations the President inherited and has not had time, really, to correct or to change?

LIPPMANN: Laos is an inheritance. We got into that. If we mismanaged it, which I think we did, the consequences have come now. That's certainly not Kennedy's fault. If he's to be criticized about that, he can be criticized either one way or the other — either by the people who think we should go to war about Laos, or by the people who say that he should never have promised to defend it. Cuba was a wrong and a foolish thing to do. It was wrong in itself. It was foolishly handled. If it had succeeded, it probably would have been worse than if it failed, because if it had succeeded, the utmost that was hoped for was that they'd get these fourteen hundred men ashore and that they'd be able to stay there. Then we'd have had a civil war which might have dragged on for weeks and weeks, with everybody getting involved in it, and no end to it.

SMITH: Now what should we do about Cuba and Castro?

LIPPMANN: The thing that put Castro overall in right perspective was a thing that Senator Fulbright

said in the private discussions beforehand, which is
that Castro is a thorn in our flesh but he's not a dagger in our hearts. The question is, is Cuba a military
threat to the United States in view of the fact that it
is so closely connected with the Soviet Union? I
would say to that, that if it were, I would call the
establishment of a missile base or a submarine base
in Cuba as marking a threat. I think we must keep
the thing under really close watch, and it's perfectly
easy to do. It's only fair to say that up to this point,
there is no evidence of any Soviet military base in
Cuba. Mr. Allen Dulles told me himself not long ago
that in the invasion there were no Russian planes;
those planes that Castro used were old American
planes. There is not a sign of a missile base, and of
course it stands to reason that if they can shoot missiles from Siberia to the moon, why should they
shoot them ninety — why should they come ninety
miles away? Anyway, we'd watch that.*

The next danger of Castro is that through his
embassies in Latin America there is a funnel through
which propaganda agents — propaganda and agents
and money gotten from the Soviet Union or China,
or somewhere — can be pushed into these various

* This broadcast was made on June 15, 1961. Soviet missiles in Cuba were not suspected until August, 1961, and
their presence was not confirmed until October, 1961.

countries of South America and the subversive propaganda supported. That is a problem about which
we can't do anything. We can't break the relations
between, let's say, Brazil and Cuba. That's up to
Brazil. But there's nothing to prevent us from watching it. Our counterintelligence ought to be good
enough to detect a good deal of it, and we ought to
keep on supplying the evidence to these governments of what's happening. But the biggest danger
of Castro — much the biggest, bigger than all these
others — is that he might succeed in Cuba in solving problems which have not yet been solved in a
great many South American-Latin American countries. That's where we have to compete with him.
If he can succeed there and our friends in other
Latin American countries fail, then his example is
far more dangerous than anything he himself can
do.

SMITH: Do you think we're on the right path toward meeting that threat?

LIPPMANN: I think we are. I think that President
Kennedy's Alliance for Progress, as he calls it — a
rather fancy name for helping — is basically right.

SMITH: Well now, the statements of most politicians come back to haunt them later, and in Kennedy's case many have come back very quickly. He
was opposed to Summit diplomacy very strongly be-

fore he was President. He was opposed to itinerant diplomacy, and yet his own men have been traveling quite a bit lately. He spoke extremely firmly about us taking a stand on Laos, which we did not take, and in fact, on Cuba. Does this indicate a quality of impulsiveness or is it standard for political statements and political behavior?

LIPPMANN: Well, take them in order. On the traveling, except for a day or two in Canada, which you really can't call traveling, they're our close neighbors, the trip that he made in June to Paris and Vienna and London was really his first trip out of the country. When you come to Dean Rusk, Secretary Rusk, there's a wholly different tale to be told, and that is a long story, I think.

SMITH: Rusk has traveled more in the same period of time, I gather, than John Foster Dulles did?

LIPPMANN: Yes. Now, the trouble with being a traveling diplomat if you're Secretary of State is that somebody else has to run the State Department. And he isn't such a wonderful diplomat that he alone can do these things. So I think he's lost the best of both worlds, so to speak. Now, in the case of John Foster Dulles, he traveled and he didn't pay attention to the State Department. He paid very little attention to it, and he let it go its own way, and he didn't give it any power. But then, the reason he did that was that he had another foreign service which operated for him, and that was his brother's Central Intelligence — CIA.

SMITH: Well, what about the CIA? Can a democracy operate an effective intelligence and espionage service?

LIPPMANN: Well, Central Intelligence, you know, is a great big grab bag of all kinds of things, and in general I would say it is absolutely indispensable to have intelligence agencies, and it has to do — it has to spy, it has to counterspy, which is almost as important as spying. It has to do a lot of operations which wouldn't look very well in print, but which every country does, such as occasionally slipping something to a politician in a very backward country, or helping an editor who'll change his mind in a backward country. And it's all very immoral, but there's no use pretending that it isn't going to be done. The trouble with CIA has been, I think — I should have said, one thing is very doubtful, whether it should ever mount expeditions like the Cuban expedition. That's so big you can't keep it secret, and therefore it's bound to fail. But really secret things are an inevitable part of government. What they did in the CIA was to take all these things and put them in one thing — everything focused on the head

of one man, who never knew whether he was trying
to tell the President what was the truth about
something or other, or what ought to be done; and
there ought to be no connection between the two.

SMITH: Well, just after the Cuban debacle, you
said that the Joint Chiefs and the head of the CIA
had to go. Do you still feel that way?

LIPPMANN: I do. I think it's going to be done too
— I hope with as little bloodshed as possible, but I
think the CIA itself may disappear and be dissolved
into its parts, taken over in different directions.

SMITH: Well, in all these setbacks in which the
CIA has been involved, the President in a speech has
implied, and many of his aides have said quite
frankly to us reporters in private, that they consider
the press to be a limitation on our effectiveness in
carrying out policy — a free press unrestrained.
What do you think about that? Do you agree with
that?

LIPPMANN: They're very confused about all that.
I think, in some ways, the press — there are some
things the press might do better or differently or not
at all than it does. But what they were complaining
about was something that happened — there's no
criticism being made of it, namely that the news of
the Cuban expedition was published to the world
before it happened. I consider it the duty of the

press to expose that kind of thing to the light of day, because I don't think a democracy like this should have secret training camps and secret armies and secret navies in foreign countries, all in violation of its treaties and its own laws.

SMITH: You once said that one of the proudest achievements of your career was that you once exposed an incident like that. Could you tell me what that was?

LIPPMANN: Well, that was many years ago when there was a grave threat of the invasion of Mexico, yes, in the twenties.

SMITH: And what did you do?

LIPPMANN: Well, I was editor of the *New York World,* and we shrieked and howled about it much more than anybody has done about Cuba, and I think we had some effect. I think we had the effect of stopping it.

SMITH: To me the chief paradox of the time we live in is that most of the resources and the skills and the wealth of the world are with the Western nations, yet the Communist nations appear to be winning the competition we call the Cold War. How do you explain that?

LIPPMANN: I think that's an exaggeration, really, and somewhat of an optical illusion. They are winning it in the most backward and reactionary places, but I don't consider that they're winning it in Europe. In spite of Castro, I don't believe they're going to win it in Brazil, which is going to determine more than anything else what happens in South America. They haven't won it in Mexico; they haven't won it in Japan. The fact that the Japanese don't love Americans doesn't mean that they're Communists.

SMITH: Well, the one question on which Khrushchev and the President seemed less pessimistic than on other questions was on Laos. Yet recent events don't seem to have borne out that relative optimism. What do you think about that?

LIPPMANN: I think the answer is that Laos is not of primary vital interest to the Soviet Union. Khrushchev regards it as quite secondary, and it's not of primary interest to the United States either. It's a country which is remote, very difficult to get at, very unsuited to American military power. There are no roads in it, no ports, no airfields, and I think that it's a wise thing for a country to tailor its policy to its military power.

SMITH: Well, do you believe in what's called the domino theory, and that is that if we lose Laos, then we'll lose South Vietnam; if we lose South Vietnam, we'll lose Thailand, and so on, until we've lost all Southeast Asia because of this one country?

LIPPMANN: I remember the domino theory first

was brought up in the Middle East, and I remember when people said Nasser made a deal with the Soviets about arms, and they said, "Ah, Egypt's gone" — then Syria was gone, and then Iraq. None of them is gone, and I don't consider Laos gone. Laos is not going to be what we rather foolishly, I think, two or three years ago tried to make it — an American satellite, whatever you like to call it. I mean, putting in a government that suited us and — that is not possible.

SMITH: Well, Mr. Lippmann, in the course of our long conversation, in which we've ranged over many subjects, you have been opposed to taking action, military, forceful action in Laos, or unilateral action in Cuba. You have said you're in favor of negotiations over Berlin, which may involve making concessions to the Russians over Berlin. What would be your answer to those who would say that this is a policy of appeasement?

LIPPMANN: My answer to that would be that you can't decide these questions of life and death for the world by epithets like appeasement. Furthermore, I think the reasons for doing what I advocate are based on the soundest strategical principle, and that is this: The Soviet Union is not engaged in any of these places. It hasn't sent its troops anywhere. As long as it isn't engaged, we mustn't be engaged. We must always keep the central power, which is the ultimate deterrent to war by the Soviet Union, intact as long as they're intact, but if we get ourselves involved in a Korean war in Indochina, and all our reserves begin flowing that way, or get ourselves involved in a thing we can't finish in Cuba because the guerrilla war may go on forever, then we will weaken ourselves for what is really the issue, which is to keep the balance of power between ourselves and the Soviet Union intact. That's the principle I have in the back of my mind in taking a position about not intervening in Laos, for example. I don't agree with the people who think that we have to go out and shed a little blood to prove we're virile men. This is too serious a business for that kind of thinking; and in regard to Cuba, my feeling was not only that, but also that it was illegal for us to do it, and we cannot go into the business of violating treaties. We're not that kind of country. And then behind that all lies a very personal and human feeling — that I don't think old men ought to promote wars for young men to fight. I don't like warlike old men. I think it's their business to try as best they can, by whatever wisdom they can find, to avert what would be an absolutely irreparable calamity for the world.

III

DECEMBER 21, 1961

Lippmann and Walter Cronkite

The balance of power was beginning to shift from the East to the West in the spring of 1961, when Walter Lippmann again visited Moscow and had the second of his day-long interviews with Khrushchev. The steady flow of refugees, many of them young and skilled, from East Germany to West Berlin was abruptly halted by the building of the Berlin Wall. At the opening of the Communist Party Twenty-second Congress, Khrushchev attacked Albania for pursuing Stalinist policies, and in the break that followed the tiny Balkan state pledged its allegiance to Red China. Dag Hammarskjold, the Secretary-General of the United Nations, negotiating for peace in Africa, was killed in an airplane crash, but two months later a cease-fire had been achieved in the Congo. President Kennedy, who was very much his own Secretary of State, had conferred with de Gaulle in Paris, with Khrushchev in Vienna, and with Macmillan in London; he had ordered the United States to resume the testing of nuclear weapons but without radioactive fallout.

CRONKITE: Mr. Lippmann, let's start with the two K's — Mr. Kennedy and Mr. Khrushchev. How is Mr. Khrushchev doing?

LIPPMANN: Well, he's obviously gotten himself into a very difficult internal position. That's what the Stalinists think. So I assume he made a whole lot of mistakes on the way, because he seemed to be in a stronger position two years ago than he is now. The position in East Germany, which is at the root of his anxieties about Berlin, has certainly been badly handled. He did not know what to do with this man, Ulbricht, who runs East Germany; so obviously that's a mess, and some attempt will have to be made to clean that up. What all the intricacies of his quarrels with the Chinese are we don't know, but there must be at the root of it the fact that he won't give them the help that they think they ought to get, and they probably feel very much about that as some people in this country feel when we build a dam in India and don't build one in some American state. They think they ought to get all the aid, and as a matter of fact, Khrushchev's giving the aid to a lot of countries that aren't even Communist.

But I think probably his biggest trouble is the fact that we forged ahead of him in nuclear weapons. I think that he started with the assumption, or had the assumption because his rockets were so good, that he was superior to us in that field, and they realized finally that they weren't, and I'm sure that shook his position in the Soviet Government, and that's why, I think, why they resumed testing in the atmosphere.

CRONKITE: Do you believe that we must resume testing in the atmosphere?

LIPPMANN: I think that's a question no layman is entitled to have an opinion about. I have great confidence in the scientific advisers to the President on this subject, particularly Dr. Hans Bethe, who knows as much about this thing as any man living in the world, and if his judgment is that we have to test, I'm willing to accept that. I don't want to be told to do it by a senator, but I'm willing to listen to him.

CRONKITE: Now, last June, in your conversation with Howard K. Smith, you said that the Kennedy administration was just a younger version of the Eisenhower administration, but you did feel that Mr. Kennedy was about to move ahead. Do you now feel that he has begun to move ahead?

LIPPMANN: Yes, decidedly — since August, I would say, decisively. And the two historic events that have opened up the new way are, one, the necessity of negotiating with the Soviet Union about the future of Berlin; and the other is the decision of the British Government to join the Common Market, which posed problems for the future of the economy of the United States of enormous magnitude. And he's moved very firmly and with great confidence in both of those openings. The Common Market problem, while it's undoubtedly the most important public question in the world today, more important than Berlin, is extremely difficult to explain, because it's so full of dry facts and uninteresting details, but there it is.

CRONKITE: Mr. Lippmann, today there is a growth in the movement that you have called the reactionary radicals. Do you think that they're becoming an important political force?

LIPPMANN: Well, I wouldn't set up to be a judge of public opinion. Other people know much more about that than I do, sitting mostly here in Washington; but my feeling is that unless the relations with the Soviet Union are kept under control diplomatically, one or the other, either the Soviet Union or somebody on our side — not necessarily the United States Government, but let's say mobs in Berlin — could precipitate a situation where nothing rational could be done about it, and that's when these groups would become very powerful. That's the danger, and that's where the Right — the radical Right, and to some extent the radical Left, in other countries would play a big and dangerous part. You see, if you follow the extremists, one goes a hundred and eighty degrees this way, and one goes a hundred and eighty degrees that way, and they meet, and they become the same thing. We've seen that all through this generation. The German Republic, which was finally overthrown by Hitler, was overthrown by a very powerful assist from the Communist Party in Germany. Then we saw that Hitler, who set up as the greatest anti-Communist of them all, was the first man to make a military alliance with Joseph Stalin — and in our own country we know plenty of people who are on the extreme Right now, and who used to be on the extreme Left. The moderate people don't swing to these extremes, and of course they're the people we count on.

CRONKITE: We see something of that kind happening in France, a splitting of the nation, it seems there, into very strongly felt emotions on the Right, and presumably there'll be a reaction from the extreme Left. How do you view France's hopes for the future?

LIPPMANN: Well, I consider the situation inside of France as very serious. To me, it's more serious than any other single situation in the world, including Berlin. And the danger in France is that the normal supports of government, beginning with the army, cannot be counted on surely to support the government. Now, how this will come out I do not know, unless General de Gaulle, as the crowning work of his life, succeeds in getting a settlement in Algeria. If he can get a settlement, then I think I can see a way where France would return to becoming a democratic republic, but short of that I'd hate to try and prophesy.

CRONKITE: Mr. Lippmann, President de Gaulle of France, whom you once rated as second only to Winston Churchill among the important figures of this century, has been the principal stumbling block to negotiating on Berlin. What do you think is behind that stubbornness?

LIPPMANN: Well, those who've known him a long time, since the World War, and have admired him, really know that when he's in a tight, difficult, weak position he becomes absolutely rigidly stubborn. And I think the explanation of the extreme difficulty of dealing with him on any subject in foreign affairs — it isn't just dealing with the Russians over Germany, it's just as bad over the UN and the Congo, and disarmament, and NATO's military force, he's out on everything — is because he's so very weak at home.

His position — he may recover his position, but his position is very weak because of Algeria.

CRONKITE: Could we possibly go into negotiations over Berlin without the French?

LIPPMANN: Yes. As a matter of fact, we have been negotiating with the Russians about Berlin since August. The talks between Secretary Rusk and Gromyko, and then with the President, are not labeled negotiations, but in fact out of them came two very important things which were negotiated, really. One was that the deadline was removed, and the other was that we would negotiate with Russia, with the Soviet Union, and not with East Germany.

CRONKITE: What do you consider negotiable on Berlin?

LIPPMANN: What is negotiable about Berlin, from our point of view, is a contract which guarantees the freedom of West Berlin, that is to say, their right to be, have their own government, elect their own government, and to have their own economic ties with the Western world — they use the German currency and all that sort of thing; and a new guarantee of access by sea, land and air to Berlin, and this guaranteed by the Soviet Union. It would not involve formal recognition of the East German state. They would be allowed to sign the agreement which we would have negotiated with the Soviet Union.

Now, you say that Bonn doesn't recognize East Germany, but ninety-five per cent of the traffic between West Berlin and the outer world — I mean to the Western world — is controlled by agreements between the West German state, Dr. Adenauer's state, and Herr Ulbricht's East German state, not at all by Allied rights.

CRONKITE: Mr. Lippmann, there's been some criticism of you and of others who support negotiation with the Soviet Union, on the basis that we can't negotiate any agreements with a nation that does not keep its pledges.

LIPPMANN: Well, I don't think that's true. John Foster Dulles negotiated an agreement with the Soviet Union for the neutralization of Austria and the evacuation of Austria, and Austria is today a free and independent, democratic country, and the Soviets haven't broken their guarantee on Austria; and they couldn't attack Austria, for example, without precipitating something like a European or a world war. And that kind of guarantee, which has that kind of physical basis, is workable. If it isn't workable, what is workable? Just let everything rot and become more and more anxious and jittery and let the mobs take over? That is no solution either. This is the age when we both have the power to destroy one another, and in such an age there is no choice but to attempt to settle the differences that remain, by diplomacy. You can't just do nothing. You have to do something.

CRONKITE: In the event that we cannot resume negotiations with the Russians on Berlin, is there anything that we could then do, unilaterally, to re-build the morale of West Berlin, so that it would again be a viable city?

LIPPMANN: We can't rebuild its prestige without giving it a subtle status in Europe, which it wouldn't have if we don't negotiate. We can pump money into West Berlin and subsidize industries there, and West Germany can do a lot; but even then the real prob-lem of West Berlin will remain with us, because the fact is that the young people are leaving Berlin, and it's becoming increasingly a city of old people, and pensioners, and so on, and there's no new blood coming in. The young blood goes out, and that is why unless we can do something drastic about it, it really is a dying city. And it cannot exist on the hope that, let us say, in twenty-five years it's going to be the capital of Germany again, although that must never be extinguished; so that is why there's a great deal to be said for the idea of putting, let's say, the European part of the United Nations, the agencies, into Berlin. That would help to make the thing more secure for one thing, because if a hundred and three nations have to go back and forth to it, the access would be open, and also there'd be a hundred and three nations witnesses as to what goes on in Berlin, which would be a good thing for Berlin, and it seems to be one of the things that it's conceivable we can come to agreement with the Soviet Union about, and that's something too.

CRONKITE: Must the wall be removed in Berlin?

LIPPMANN: The wall will have to be removed some day, of course, and I hope it won't take twenty-five years to remove it. It can't be kicked down because that's a fighting matter. That's one of those acts like driving people into a corner where you go perfectly irrational. But the thing could melt. The exits could be increased, and the crossings of it. The thing could be allowed to get out of repair and they don't replace the rusty barbed wire. That sort of thing could happen if you get some kind of a workable agreement about the future of Berlin. It should be taken for granted in all negotiations and we should all say that this thing is a monstrosity as such, but it's a fact, and we can't say, we are not in a position in Berlin to say, "Remove the wall or else." Because what's "else"?

CRONKITE: Could we have knocked down the wall at the time it was being built, do you think?

LIPPMANN: Well, nobody thought of doing it and

nobody — I mean, General de Gaulle didn't think of it and didn't say so, and Dr. Adenauer not only didn't think of it but went on making campaign speeches in the other part of Germany. Nobody thought of it at first, and I think once it got started, any really — any military move against it would certainly have been met by a military move from the Soviet side. They couldn't possibly accept the humiliation of letting American tanks crush this wall, and they stand by and let it happen.

CRONKITE: Mr. Lippmann, do you think it was a failure on the part of the administration not to have foreseen the possibility of this wall being built in Berlin?

LIPPMANN: Well, yes. Now, this will be very strongly denied in the administration. They did know that it was one of the possible things to do. There's no doubt about it. The Intelligence said that this was one of the things cooking, but where we failed — and it's not only we alone but all the Allies, our allies in Britain and France, and so forth — where we failed is to anticipate how important the wall would be.

CRONKITE: Changing the subject just a little bit, the whole crisis in Berlin brought us to another crisis of our own making in this country, that surrounding fallout shelters. Do you agree with the opinion of some that the whole discussion of fallout shelters creates the idea that there is a possibility of survival in an atomic war, and therefore might even sponsor an atomic war?

LIPPMANN: Well, yes, but first of all it's a delusion. There is no shelter program that can possibly be built, carried out in the foreseeable near future, which would possibly be a real protection against a full-scale nuclear war. And therefore, it's a bad thing to excite people in something that deceives them. Now, there is no protection against nuclear war except to prevent it. And I think we're quite capable of doing that unless we go crazy and take impossible positions.

CRONKITE: Well, how can we prevent it?

LIPPMANN: Because we have a power to strike back even if we're struck first, and that prevents a country being hit except irrationally; we never can forget that the world does go crazy at times.

CRONKITE: Well, Mr. Lippmann, we seem constantly to be on the defensive around the world. How can we take the offensive for a change?

LIPPMANN: I'd say we should put our minds on solving our own — taking advantage of our own opportunities, and the biggest one of all there, of course, is to work out, in the Western world or the non-Communist world, around the Common Market,

enlarged by Great Britain, joined by the Commonwealth, and in some relation with the United States
and Latin America, a great low-tariff trading area.
Now, we're just started on that, and the administration is going to make that the main issue, the main
theme of the next session of Congress, and if we
ever pull that off, as I think we can, it will make the
West so rich and so powerful — I don't mean in
number of megaton bombs, because that we could
do anyway — but so powerful in its influence, that
it will tend to act like an enormous magnet on Eastern Europe. Austria wants to come in. All right,
Austria's a neutral. Finland would like to come in;
it's a different kind of neutral. But here you have
this great movement on foot which is going to unite
in some kind of common economic trading area,
Western Europe, the British Commonwealth, North
and South America, and Australia — Australasia
— Australia and New Zealand, and Japan. That's an
enormous thing. It's incomparably more powerful
and richer than the Soviet bloc.

CRONKITE: Mr. Lippmann, is there some hope
that the people of West Germany would look toward
this Common Market as their great hope rather than
toward reunification with East Germany?

LIPPMANN: Under Adenauer, and until recently,

they were allowed to believe — encouraged to believe that they could have all that and also have reunification. And it's been a great shock to them, this year, to realize that isn't going to happen, and that really, for a long time to come, probably for at least a generation, they have got to make the choice which they've already made, of uniting with the West rather than of uniting with East Germany.

CRONKITE: Mr. Lippmann, you said some time earlier that you felt that Cuba would eventually, and in the not too distant future, come back into the American community. Now that Castro admits he's a Communist, do you still feel that way?

LIPPMANN: Yes, because I don't regard Castro as something permanent. I think this last exhibition — I think he's really — I felt it the first time I saw him, the only time I ever saw him when he came up to Washington a year and a half ago — that the man is demented. This isn't a powerful, iron-willed, calculating force of nature such as a great — this is a rather demented man. Those men do not come to a good end, and this last performance when he announced he was a Communist, whether he had been or not, he may have been not telling the truth even — not sure. Certainly, it didn't please the Soviet Union any, because what he was doing really was calling on them for help — a sort of a drowning man's plea, so I don't think the Castro thing has got a long life ahead of it.

CRONKITE: If we could turn for a moment, Mr. Lippmann, to the Congo — would you make any prediction as to the outcome there?

LIPPMANN: I couldn't make a prediction except in this sense. The Congo is insolvable without the agreement of the major Western powers. Now, we know the Soviet Union is opposed. We can't count on that — it won't help us, but we must have the support particularly of Great Britain, and that should bring with it Belgium, and if by some good luck we could get France, then there would be a chance of working out some kind of conciliation in which the Congo could go on, more or less, under some kind of a nursemaid over it, because it's not capable of self-government now.

My nightmare about this whole business is twofold. First that all of Africa from Katanga south, which includes Rhodesia, Portuguese Angola, and the Union of South Africa, will become the last stand of the European white man in the continent, and very powerful. This will rouse up all Africa north of that — and I'm not talking about the Mediterranean, but what is known as dark Africa — black Africa — against it, and it will get the support of the Soviet Union. So you stand in great danger of a struggle between the Western — the European — countries and the Soviet Union, and between black and white, and the combination would be a witches' brew which we must try to avert. And that is the ultimate justification for Hammarskjold's policy in the Congo. I think what he did, and was trying to do when he died, will be remembered longer and talked about longer than any of the events which fill up the headlines day by day, because in that lies the attempt which may fail in the Congo but which will be revived in some other way, some other place — to impose conciliation and peace in a situation which might lead to the most dreadful catastrophe of war.

IV

Lippmann and David Schoenbrun

In April, 1962, Mr. Lippmann made one of his periodic visits to the European capitals. In Rome he talked with Prime Minister Amintore Fanfani; Ugo La Malfa, minister of the budget; and Pietro Nenni, the leader of the Italian Socialists. In Brussels he met with Foreign Minister Paul Henri Spaak; in Berlin he saw General Lucius Clay and Mayor Willy Brandt; in London he interviewed various members of the Cabinet including R. A. B. Butler; Edward Heath, then conducting negotiations with the Common Market; Lord Home; Harold Caccia of the Foreign Office, and Hugh Gaitskell, leader of the Labor opposition; and in Paris he had one of his most rewarding talks with General Charles de Gaulle.

SCHOENBRUN: Mr. Lippmann, a year ago you returned from Russia and reviewed the world situation, and now you've just returned from Western Europe. Many things have changed in this past year. Would you review the situation now?

LIPPMANN: I think there are signs that would permit one to say that the balance of forces between East and West has shifted somewhat in favor of the West. When I say shift in our favor, I don't mean that the situation has shifted the way we'd like it to shift everywhere in the world. What I mean is that as between the two great blocs, the coalitions that confront one another — the Communist coalition and the Western coalition — the balance of forces, military, political, economic and psychological, is rather more favorable to us than it was, or seemed to be six months ago. We have developed the power, through various measures we've taken, to survive any attack that the Soviets could make on us with such a devastating reply that they'll never make the attack; and it is now universally recognized in Europe, as far as I can make out, that that is the situation, and one of the signs of this change is that it's a long time since anybody talked about a shelter in this country.

SCHOENBRUN: If the balance of power is turning in our favor, just how do you determine that?

LIPPMANN: First of all, the period when we felt that we were in danger of being struck, which is the period you know when people were talking about the so-called missile gap, and when the Soviet was supposed to be powerful enough to knock out our whole military establishment in one great blow — we now know that that was an absolutely false estimate. We were the victims, in part, of mistaken intelligence, which I must say at once did not come from Allen Dulles and the CIA, but probably from the Air Force. But anyway, the country was tremendously taken over, and of course, as you remember it, it went into the campaign and all that. Well, we now know that isn't true. That never existed. The Soviets never built the missiles that they were supposed to be able to build, and we didn't have the knowledge of what exists inside the Soviet Union that we have today. And one of the evidences of how much better our intelligence is appears in something that sounds rather technical. Our strategy in nuclear war is no longer based on the idea of just destroying Russian cities, but of destroying the actual striking power of the Soviet Union, and that takes a lot of good intelligence, and we seem to have it.

SCHOENBRUN: Mr. Lippmann, what's the thing that has convinced us, and maybe even the Russians, that things have changed?

LIPPMANN: I think the best proof that the estimate is accepted in Moscow, not merely in Paris and Bonn and in Washington, is that they resumed nuclear testing. They resumed nuclear testing because they knew they were behind us in nuclear power. And they were told — Khrushchev undoubtedly was told by his scientists and his military men that if they made one more, or two more series of tests, they might get a great breakthrough. They might be able to develop an anti-missile missile, or some kind of bomb that was so powerful that nothing could stop it, and in one shot it would finish everything. And I think it's like that. I think that's the best proof that they know. Well, the other proof is that they really have become much more prudent in their dealings with us, both in Berlin and Germany, and in Southeast Asia, for example.

SCHOENBRUN: You're suggesting, it seems to me, that something must be happening with the Soviet thinking?

LIPPMANN: Well, I wouldn't like to pretend to say

what their thinking is, but if we take what the facts are, and the balance of forces, it isn't only this military matter which we've been talking about, but economically they see Europe becoming a very prosperous and rich society, and not Communist, not even Socialist, and the example of the recovery of Europe and its really great booming condition is a very impressive example all over the world for small countries that are not well developed, or are very much underdeveloped. They can see that this can be done. They can become rich not by being like the United States, which nobody can imitate, and not by imitating the Soviets, which they don't want to imitate, but by a method which the Europeans, small countries and large, and not merely Common Market countries, but Austria, for example, and the Scandinavian — they are all showing that there is a way to raise the standard of life and become richer, and so on, which is neither one or the other. The example of this thing is very impressive everywhere, and it constitutes much more than any amount of making anti-Communist speeches and denouncing this and that and the other thing. It exerts an influence on the thinking of people who have to run governments all over the world.

SCHOENBRUN: If the affluent society in Europe is evidence that the tide is turning in our favor, does it follow, then, that Communism has been stopped in Western Europe?

LIPPMANN: Well, yes, in all of Western Europe, the Communist parties have lost their connection with Moscow as instruments, and the left-wing parties, including the more moderate — even the moderate Socialists find themselves living in a continent where socialism is out of date. Europe has outlived socialism. And you go and talk to the French Socialists, talk to the British Labourites, German Social Democrats, they're wondering what does socialism do now that its period is over. It'll go on, because the world needs people who are not conservatively interested only on the side of property, but are on the side of people who don't have property — and the farmers — but the decline of socialism in Europe is a very striking thing.

SCHOENBRUN: Now, with this point you're making about the decline of Communism and socialism, perhaps you could talk to us a bit about what's happening inside the Communist bloc. What are their stresses and strains?

LIPPMANN: Well, there are a good many. The biggest stress and strain comes from agriculture — the agricultural failures. A country like Poland manages to escape that only by not being Communist in its agriculture, and that's pretty well evident to everybody in the Eastern bloc. And then, of course, in China it's a terrific disaster, so great that it's producing a famine, and we don't begin to know what the consequences inside China will be, but we know it's very serious. We know that even in the Soviet Union, where it's not so bad and where people are not hungry, it's still sufficiently a failure so that they have no exports. Russia used to be a wheat exporting country. Well, today it is really not able to help China, for example, its ally. That makes a very great difference. Most of the people who live on this planet live on the land and live by farming of one kind or another, and to see the Communist countries with shortages of food, while in the Western world and in Canada and Australia, and South America, you have surpluses of food — that's a tremendously impressive spectacle, and it's part of what you might call the turning of the tide.

Then, it's quite clear that the younger intellectual generation, the young students and the people who are coming out of their universities, and under forty, and their artists and poets, are very tired of being shut out of the world and want to make contact with the Western world. Very hungry for it. And they are pressing Khrushchev very hard to liberalize the regime more than — he's liberalized it a great deal as compared with Stalin, but it's still a long way from being a liberal regime, and they want to liberalize it more, and that's where his greatest internal pressure comes from, I think.

SCHOENBRUN: In your trip around Western Europe, I'm sure that you spoke with many Soviet diplomats. What explanation do they give about American-Russian relations today?

LIPPMANN: Well, I was talking to one not long ago, and I said — I asked him, "What would you say was the biggest change that's occurred in our relations? They're obviously not as dangerous as they were a year or two ago." And we both accepted the impossibility of nuclear war between us, and so on. And he said, "Oh, I think I can tell you." This was a fairly young man, but very important. He said, "I think I can tell you. We both have gotten over the idea that the other is omnipotent." I said, "Well, explain that." And he said, "When anything went wrong in the world that we didn't like, in Russia, we said, 'That's Washington and Wall Street, and they just manipulated.' No matter where it was, Nigeria, any place; and you, when anything went wrong, said, 'Well, that's made in Moscow.' As a matter of fact, we can't even run China or Albania, much less the world, and we know that we are not omnipotent and we know that you aren't."

SCHOENBRUN: Mr. Lippmann, you've seen all the

leaders of Europe — most recently, de Gaulle. Do you find that the Europeans are more aware of this shifting balance of power, and take it into account in their policy?

LIPPMANN: Yes. You take, for instance, the attitude of General de Gaulle and Chancellor Adenauer on dealing with Berlin. Now, they may be right or wrong about this or that in it, but they feel perfectly confident that they can defy the Soviet Union without precipitating a nuclear war. Well, why? Not because they have any power. It's because we've got that power.

SCHOENBRUN: Well, why does General de Gaulle ask for more nuclear weapons? I'm sure you must have discussed that with him. What kind of power is he looking for?

LIPPMANN: The French nuclear striking force which he is beginning to build up is, by American standards and by Soviet standards, negligible. It's something in the ratio of perhaps fifty to three thousand, somewhere in that order of importance, and that's going to take years to produce. It doesn't exist now. It has two purposes. They both are political and they both have to do with Washington — not with Moscow. He thinks if he gets the kind of force he believes he can get in some years, and that if he decided that bombs had to be used in the

European conflict, he could do it; and of course, we'd have to come in and finish it, but he could start it — and that's, by the way, a power we're never going to give him. And the other is that if we got into a nuclear war, say, in the Far East, where France is not interested, he might be sufficiently too hot to handle to be dealt with directly by the Soviet power, and therefore might be able to sit it out. It's all political speculation — not really military reasoning.

SCHOENBRUN: Well, General de Gaulle has used that technique for the last twenty years, and every time he has, it's because he's judged the world situation has provided an opportunity for France. Would you suggest that your own theory that the tide is now running in our favor is General de Gaulle's analysis too?

LIPPMANN: Basically, yes. It's running sufficiently in our favor so that it has become possible to make a contest for the leadership of the West. Remember, during the world war — World War II — the tide of battle began to turn after Stalingrad and the British victories in North Africa, but as soon as the tide began to turn, the rivalry within the anti-Nazi coalition — between Great Britain and Russia, and the United States — broke out as to who was going to make the peace. Well, that's a little bit far-fetched, the analogy. You mustn't always reason from analogy, but still, something like that is what is happening today in Europe and in the world.

SCHOENBRUN: As you see the tide running in our favor now, would you say that to a large extent, for Europeans, that the Common Market is their magnificent Stalingrad?

LIPPMANN: Well, for those Europeans who belong to the Common Market, which is only six out of I don't know how many — fifteen, sixteen countries. The thing is that Europe has recovered — that it's now a booming, affluent society, of which the Common Market is a very important expression and will be more so if it can be enlarged. But the change in Europe's feeling that on the one hand war has been deterred — nuclear war, and therefore other kinds of war, really, as far as Europe is concerned; and that it is now able to raise its own standard of life, has found the way to do this — yes, that marks the change, if you want to call it, the Stalingrad.

SCHOENBRUN: Well, then, is General de Gaulle striking out for leadership of this prosperous Common Market in European society — at this opportunity now?

LIPPMANN: Yes, General de Gaulle believes that France, as of historic right, should be the leader of Europe, and from General de Gaulle's point of view, Great Britain is not part of Europe. When you ask him about Great Britain, he says, "No, that's an island." What he's talking about is Europe on the Continent. Another point about it is, we have to remember, for him, Europe begins at the Atlantic and extends to the Urals. In other words, it includes most of what is now Russia. And I know, I'm sure, because he said this many times, his vision is of a Europe led by France, with great statesmanship and wisdom, power and so on, coming eventually to a Europe which extends and includes the Soviet Union and all of Eastern Europe and all that. That's the vision.

SCHOENBRUN: Mr. Lippmann, in a previous talk of this kind with Howard K. Smith, didn't you once say that General de Gaulle was perhaps one of the greatest men — one of the greatest leaders in the world?

LIPPMANN: I did.

SCHOENBRUN: Do you still feel that way about him?

LIPPMANN: I do. He's one of the greatest men of our time, and I must say, when you see him, he hasn't lost any of his fascination. He's a fascinating talker and all that. But that doesn't mean he's always right, and I think he's wrong in his conception of Europe, especially since it involves the exclu-

sion of Great Britain from Europe, and the exclusion of Great Britain means the exclusion of Scandi-
navia and a tight little Europe, organized around
France and Germany. I think that's a wrong conception, and it wouldn't be the first time that somebody differed with a very great man. I don't think
that he's any less a very great man.

SCHOENBRUN: He's a very difficult man to differ
with, as President Kennedy has discovered.

LIPPMANN: He is. He doesn't — as far as I know
him, and my experience with him goes over many
years — he never argues anything. He pronounces it.

SCHOENBRUN: If the balance is now in our favor,
where does that leave us with the great unsolved
problems of the world — Berlin, Laos, China? Perhaps we can begin with Berlin.

LIPPMANN: Both sides have recognized the existence of the stalemate. That's the big change in
the past year there. You remember that a year
ago, when the President saw Khrushchev in Vienna,
that was in June a year ago, he came away with the
distinct impression that Khrushchev was going to use
force of some kind to compel West Berlin — to make
us give up West Berlin. And there was an ultimatum
at the time — you remember that it had to be done
by the thirty-first of December, and if it wasn't done

by the thirty-first of December, he was going to make
a separate treaty with the East German Republic,
and they were going to strangle the access, and
he was going to back them up; and so everybody
said, "Let's build shelters for the war that's coming."
Well, what happened? Two things happened. First
of all, he didn't strangle Berlin. He cut off East Berlin and Eastern Germany from the West, by building
the wall across Berlin. Just the opposite of a blockade; and on the other hand, he withdrew the ultimatum. He took the time limit away, and once that happened, the fuse was taken out of the Berlin crisis,
and we were in then for what we've got — a long
period of talk. We, on the other hand, gave up,
although we never said so — we accepted the wall.
We didn't try to push it over as some people think we
should have tried; but the answer to that is, of
course, that the Russians would have built it one
street back, and then we would have had to invade
them to knock it down the second time. We accepted
it, protesting, but we accepted the fact that that was
the way the world was, and they were able to live
with that situation. Now, we've got to do that. It's not
nice. The wall is a horrible thing to look at, and
some day it'll come down, and some day the two Ber-
lins and the two Germanys will come together again,
coalesce; but that time isn't now and we are living,

both of us, Soviet Union and the West, with the fact that that's the way it is, and we're not going to have a nuclear war about it.

SCHOENBRUN: Well, why is it necessary to negotiate? Why don't we just sit still on the status quo?

LIPPMANN: Because it isn't safe. You see, Berlin is one of the places in the world where Soviet and American troops are just across the street from each other. It's the only place. Other places, there's a big, empty space somewhere between them and — here it's too dangerous. Somebody could start something, a scuffle or a row, or a captain gets drunk, or something, and then — the tanks would begin to come up. We'd put up tanks and then they'd put up tanks and then somebody shoots, and we have to avoid that. At least, we have to be talking; and as long as we don't have an agreement with the Russians, we have to be on talking terms with them, so that in case some trouble comes, we can always explain it to each other.

SCHOENBRUN: Would you care to hazard a guess as to what price the Soviets would be willing to accept for an accommodation in Berlin?

LIPPMANN: Well, yes, you don't mean a final settlement, but an accommodation by which we could live without being worried from day to day whether there's going to be another Berlin crisis. Basically, it's the degree of recognition which we're willing to give to the East German state.

SCHOENBRUN: There is such bitterness on both sides of the wall, such hatred in the West for the East Germans. Could we possibly grant them any degree of recognition?

LIPPMANN: Well, we can't give them and won't, of course, give them formal recognition in the sense of exchanging ambassadors with them and so on; but, of course, you know there's a great deal of recognition already. You take all the trade between West Germany and West Berlin. It comes by road, it comes by railroad, it comes by canal. That's all controlled now by agreements between West Germany and East Germany. If you like, between Dr. Adenauer and Mr. Ulbricht, and that is ninety-five per cent of all the traffic between Berlin and the West. The part that is really being argued about is the five per cent, which is based on our military rights there as the victors in the war, and that's where Khrushchev is raising questions now that we're negotiating.

SCHOENBRUN: I wonder why Dr. Adenauer gets so angry every time Americans talk about negotiations?

LIPPMANN: He doesn't — he cannot agree to anything that seems to fix and sign and seal the permanent partition of Germany. That's what it's about, and it's perfectly understandable. It's perfectly natural that he should feel that way.

SCHOENBRUN: It seems to me that Dr. Adenauer's bitterness, his intensity of feeling, must be based on something more than just the fear of partition. There must be other roots to it, wouldn't you think?

LIPPMANN: Oh, well, there is such a — yes, there is an emotional basis for it. You know, the fact is that Dr. Adenauer has become a very old man, and a very old man doesn't like the things he's used to to change, and he became used — when John Foster Dulles was Secretary of State, and even before that, when Acheson was Secretary of State — to being the most consulted man in Europe on European affairs by the United States. Well, he isn't that any longer and that is a hard thing to get used to, and the fact that he isn't always the first consulted, that we also consult the British, and we consult other countries in Europe, makes him very suspicious. He thinks things are being arranged behind his back, which isn't so — nothing is being arranged behind his back. We don't make a move that we don't tell him about, but he's irritable and suspicious about it.

SCHOENBRUN: Well, isn't it always true that when we do make a move and consult him, that we often quarrel with him perhaps more than we did in the past?

LIPPMANN: Yes, because we are trying to get an accommodation about Berlin — we were talking about, you know, something that will work for a few years until the day comes when we can begin seriously to deal with the question of the reunification of Germany, not by abolishing East Germany, but by making the two coalesce and grow back together into one nation; and that day won't come while Dr. Adenauer is in office, and it won't come while Ulbricht is in office in East Germany. But when those two men go, and I don't know when that'll be, it will begin, because the pull of union between them is very much stronger than any other force and will prevail.

SCHOENBRUN: Is it your opinion that there is really a different American policy vis-à-vis Germany and Europe, and not only a different attitude?

LIPPMANN: There's no different policy on anything essential. This administration is just as committed as the one before to keeping American troops in Berlin, keeping the air corridors and the others open to access, and we'll go to as great lengths as anybody. The President, last July, thought he was on the verge of war over the thing and was prepared to face it. Nothing has changed in that respect. We haven't given up any of the vital interests

of the German people, which are our interests too in
a sense, but we cannot tack and zigzag our policy
to suit German internal politics, as we have in the
past. Now Germany, inside, is not nearly as inflexible
as Dr. Adenauer makes it sound, and we know
that and we're interested in a lot of Germans, both
on the Right and the Left, and in the Center in his
own party; we see them and talk to them. And that
is disturbing, of course, but it doesn't represent a
radical change unless you want to regard it as a radical change from having a one-man relationship.

SCHOENBRUN: Well, if the tide is changing, just
where does this leave the third area — Africa?

LIPPMANN: I think we have succeeded — well,
that sounds too boastful. I think it has happened,
through good luck and good management, that
Africa will not become the scene of a great conflict
between the Soviet Union and the United States.
That's been pushed out of it. The instrument, of
course, has been the United Nations in the Congo. I
don't think the Soviet Union is now in the position to
intervene in any effective, important way in Africa.
It's too far away. Her wealth isn't great enough. Her
military reach isn't great enough; and I think if
that's played wisely, we have averted that. Now,
that doesn't mean that the problems are settled,
because what's going on in Africa, and to some de-

gree also in, say, Indochina, or Southeast Asia, as it's now called, and there's other parts of the world, Latin America, to some degree, is something that didn't start in Moscow and it didn't start in Washington. It started right in the soil of the country. It's a revolutionary condition. Just as, why could there be a revolution in Russia? There was no Russia to start the revolution in Russia. Those things grow out of the soil and that will go on, even if we do get to reasonably good coexistence with the Soviet Union and get China hedged in, and so on, still, that'll go on. Africa will probably be in a turbulent state for a hundred years.

SCHOENBRUN: I wonder if you could talk to us a bit about Southeast Asia, and the great danger spot that's in the news all the time — Laos.

LIPPMANN: The most important thing about Laos is to know where it is, and Laos is a country which has no harbors. It's locked inside of Southeast Asia. It's a country which was created fifteen years ago, or less. There never was a Laos before, and it has no nationality, just collections of tribes and feudal lords and princes, and so on, and it is the neighbor of China. It borders on China and it borders on North Vietnam, which is the part of Vietnam that stayed in Communist hands, under Ho Chi Minh, so in the norm of things, you'd expect that China would

be the great country acting in Laos, but what we
find is, that Russia is the country that is acting.
Now, Russia is almost as far away from Laos as we
are. They've got to come all the way around and it's
not easy for them to get there, just as it isn't easy
for us. It's easier for us, maybe, than for them.
And the question is, what are the Russians after?
Why are they so interested? Not because they think
Laos would be a gold mine for them if they could
somehow or other put up a Communist — Russian
Communist — government there. The country is a
miserable affair. No use to them — anybody. It's a
liability. I think they are there to keep the Chinese
from coming in, and I think their object there is,
primarily, to prevent the Chinese, who are reck-
less and inexperienced, from doing something that
would produce a war between the United States
and China, just as we had one in Korea. They don't
want this because they don't want to be in a position where they'd either have to abandon their ally,
which would be very difficult, as a Communist, or
they'd have to get into a war with the United States,
which would be even worse. So I think they're in
there for preventive reasons, and if there's any hope
of getting any kind of a working arrangement —
it's pretty hard to deal with these people to get anything to stick, because they promise something and

then it goes unstuck the next day — it's because we and the Russians have agreed that neither of us wants to be in Laos provided the other stays out, and that means a neutral Laos.

SCHOENBRUN: How do you evaluate the President's decision in sending armed forces into Thailand?

LIPPMANN: I think it all is related to the hope and belief that we have a basic understanding with the Russians about Laos. If so, it's about the equivalent in the old days of sending a gunboat to some place that's in trouble. They're not there to fight anybody, and whether it's good to send a gunboat or not is an arguable question. It all depends on whether our judgment of the real relations, which I tried to describe, with Russia is correct.

SCHOENBRUN: There's a very different situation, of course, in South Vietnam, where there's a war going on. How do you evaluate that?

LIPPMANN: I don't think the Russians have any great interest in making South Vietnam Communist, and I don't think they greatly resent our helping the Vietnamese to defend themselves against the guerrillas, because they are old-fashioned in their views of diplomacy, and that's our sphere of influence, and we're behind the line, and the interesting thing about Vietnam is how little they have protested about it. They begged through a formal statement, but otherwise they didn't do anything.

SCHOENBRUN: Isn't that also —

LIPPMANN: Whether our policy will work, nobody can say. I couldn't say today, certainly. We're trying to do something extremely difficult, which is to make a very unsatisfactory government work — be acceptable to the people of this country, and I don't know whether that'll do.

SCHOENBRUN: Perhaps we can make a quick jump to another part of the world — to Cuba. You suggested about a year ago that we were making too much of a fuss about Mr. Castro. He really wasn't a very important fellow, just let him alone and he'd fall down. How do you feel about Mr. Castro today?

LIPPMANN: I feel more than ever — I think it's worked fine. Castro is much less important than he was a year ago. His prestige in South America has gone down. His power to harm us has proved to be negligible. We have problems enough in South America, but they don't come from Castro.

SCHOENBRUN: Let me ask you this, Mr. Lippmann. Could you evaluate this Kennedy administration now? What has it succeeded in doing? What has it failed to do?

LIPPMANN: I would say that since last summer,

since the administration, so to speak, collected
itself after the shock of Cuba first, and then the
shock of the meeting with Khrushchev in Vienna,
and the building of the wall, and so on, and began
to reassess its military power and its economic power,
the style has been very good, I mean, the tide is favorable, and Kennedy is proving, I think, a very admirable mariner, a navigator in that kind of sea. Instead of using his great power to threaten and to
make himself tougher, he has used it to promote an
accommodating policy, which, of course, improves
his position; and I consider that very successful, because he knows that there's no such thing as victory
in a nuclear war, and so he doesn't talk about it, and
doesn't try to act as if he thought it was possible, so
on that side it's very good.

Now, in the Alliance he is faced with problems
that are very difficult, because what is really happening there is that while our military supremacy or
leadership, let's say, pre-eminence, inside the Alliance is undisputable, nobody can touch it. The
course — it'd be utterly beyond Europe to challenge
it. Our economic and financial pre-eminence in the
world, relative to Europe, is declining. Our great
creditor position in the world has, of course, been
liquidated through wise policies — the Marshall
Plan and foreign aid, and so on, so that we no

longer have a surplus of gold, which we can sort of feed out to the world to restore it. And we have done that, and it's been one of the great — historically I think it will be regarded as one of the great disinterested achievements of a nation after a great war; and without it Europe's recovery could not have taken place. I don't say it took place because of it — it would not have taken place without it. Now it's becoming a serious drain on us. That's very important from the European point of view. They are much more powerful, financially, than we are. They have surpluses and we have deficits.

Then, another thing that plays a very great role is the fact that they have found ways, through financial policy and tax policy, and so on, budget policy, to produce much higher rates of economic growth than we have. We conduct a fiscal policy, have been conducting it under President Eisenhower, and we continued under President Kennedy, which does not fit the growth of the modern world, the growth of the economy in the modern world; and under President Eisenhower we had three recessions, and each recovery from a recession lasted a shorter time than the preceding one. Now, we've had a permanent mass of unemployment and underuse of capital plant. We've been running way below our potential, and at a growth rate which has

been around three per cent, which is very low compared to any other great industrial power in the
world. This has not been corrected under Kennedy.
Mr. Kennedy has made moves during the recession
to alleviate distress in certain areas, to raise some
palliatives, but the basic condition, the basic financial policy of prematurely balancing the budget,
which is what I think he has done, is based on the
fact that if he doesn't do that, he will be attacked
by the Republicans and by a large part of the Democrats as irresponsible, disreputable, and so on. We
are throttling our own development by a refusal to
allow the economy to have enough stimulus from
public as well as private investment, to keep going
at a high rate.

SCHOENBRUN: I wonder if you could be specific
about that. What should we do that we aren't doing?

LIPPMANN: I would go this far as to say that the
immediate thing to do is to make a drastic reduction — a very severe and substantial reduction in direct taxes on incomes and corporation, and that will
unbalance the budget, not merely the budget that
everybody talks about, but the real balance of pay-
ments between the different parts of the economy,
favorably. It will act as a stimulus and that is not
merely a shot in the arm — that's really nourish-
ment for the economy. I think we're trying to make

too big a part of our tax revenues come by direct taxes, by income taxes, and I think the people feel the weight of that when they have to pay into it, where they don't feel indirect taxes like the gasoline tax and tobacco tax, and so on. I think we've gone beyond the endurable limits of direct taxation, and I think it causes a lot of political unrest in this country, too.

SCHOENBRUN: Do you think that it's possible, with all the tremendous burdens of our commitments at home and abroad, to cut government income, or to replace direct taxes by indirect, or is there some other way of generating the means for our commitments?

LIPPMANN: Well, if we can raise our annual rate of economic growth from three and a half, to four or four and a half, let's say, the income that'll generate will, under lower taxes, produce more revenue. It'll mean that we'll produce probably thirty or forty billion dollars a year more wealth than we do now. And that'll pay for all of these things. We're a country that is trying to carry tremendous burdens, defense and foreign aid, and nuclear weapons, and all that sort of thing, and operating way under its capacity, and that isn't possible. The weight — the thing gets too heavy a burden on the people, because they have to spend too much out of too little product.

A country where steel capacity, steel production is running something like sixty per cent of capacity and where there is unemployment in the labor force of five — five and a half — per cent is not able to take on the burdens of leadership and pre-eminence in the world as it is today.

SCHOENBRUN: How do you evaluate the President's fight with U. S. Steel?

LIPPMANN: The real cause of the violence of the flare-up over the steel increase was based not so much on economic considerations, in my view. It was based on what looked like bad faith. The steel company kept back its announcement of price increases until every union had been signed up for a year, so it couldn't increase wages, and then it announced the price increase. That wasn't playing ball, and the President was put in the position of having made labor take less than it wanted, on the assumption that prices wouldn't increase. He was made to look as if he deceived them, and I think that's the cause of the emotional flare-up. Now, there were certain things he did in that, which I didn't altogether like. I didn't like bringing the FBI into it, to call up newspapermen, and of course I'm a newspaperman, in the middle of the night, to ask them questions about the steel business. That was excessive, and was bad judgment, and caused a bad reaction, but of course it has nothing to do with the main issue. If the steel companies had been able to raise the price of steel after the settlement with the trade unions, we would have had an impossible situation with trade unions all over the country, and maybe the President reacted too angrily, but he had to react. He had no choice in the matter. They gave him no choice.

SCHOENBRUN: Did the steel crisis have any effect on the stock market sag?

LIPPMANN: No. I think it's absolutely certain it is not the cause of it, because the bear market, the fall in the stock market prices began, this is a matter of fact, on the sixteenth of March. The explosion with steel — the steel thing broke out on the eleventh of April, or the tenth — eleventh or tenth of April. Before that, nothing had happened with steel except everything was going well, so that obviously the steel thing didn't start the bear market. Now, the bear market has gone on since steel — maybe it's gotten a little sharper, but I think the reasons for the bear market are not because Mr. Blough felt hurt, or somebody felt sorry that Mr. Blough had been handled so roughly, it's because the underlying conditions as to what our recovery from the recession of '61 is going to be, and what the possibilities of another recession next year are, point to a bear market.

SCHOENBRUN: Perhaps we could talk about some of the people around the President. For example, it has been suggested that it was not the President who sent the FBI around to call people at three and four in the morning, but it was his brother Bobby. How do you evaluate the Attorney General?

LIPPMANN: The Attorney General, Bobby, is a very attractive human being, but he is — his greatest weakness, I'm afraid, the thing that I worried about before he was appointed — is that when he's bent on what he thinks is the right course, he's rather ruthless in action, and I think this FBI thing was an example of that. And I assume it was he — it must have been he, because he's the boss of that.

SCHOENBRUN: Well, now, what about some of the other people in the Cabinet? Secretary of Defense McNamara and Dean Rusk — could you talk about them?

LIPPMANN: Well, Dean Rusk has proved himself, I think, since, roughly speaking, last summer, to be a really first-class negotiator with the Russians. He's got one quality that is indispensable for dealing with the Russians. He never gets bored. He can say the same thing and listen to the same thing. The Russians say the same thing ten times in the course of an hour. He can listen to it and say his thing ten times, and he says this himself, and it's a great quality. And therefore I think he's been a very successful negotiator with the Russians. His negotiations with Gromyko, at the end of August I think it was, after the wall business, resulted really in taking the ultimatum out of the Berlin situation.

SCHOENBRUN: What about the Secretary of Defense, Mr. McNamara?

LIPPMANN: McNamara — Secretary McNamara is the ablest man who has come into the Pentagon since it was built. He's the man who more than any man who's ever occupied the post, understands the whole problem just as well as any general does, and he's quite able to talk to the generals and the colonels and the strategists in the Pentagon on even terms. They can't just talk down to him as a layman. The result is that you have what we're supposed to have in this country — civilian control of the military in a way that I don't think we've had it since the war.

SCHOENBRUN: One of the big decisions that Mr. McNamara had a big part in was our decision to resume nuclear testing. How do you feel about that?

LIPPMANN: Well, we did that to reinsure ourselves against a Soviet breakthrough.

SCHOENBRUN: There was a great split inside this administration on whether we should resume testing or not. Do you think that the President himself

exercised complete leadership, that it was his decision alone?

LIPPMANN: Yes, I do. I think it's one of the most
admirable performances, because he really did study
the thing and listened to it, and went through all
the agonies of this awfully technical and hard thing
to understand. He's not a lazy man — President Kennedy.

SCHOENBRUN: Mr. Lippmann, you've been telling
us the tide is turning in our favor. A lot of citizens
in this country would really disagree with you.
There's Laos in which we look very bad. There's
Turkey uncertain. Algeria blowing up. France in
trouble. Brazil. Argentina. What do you say to people who are genuinely worried about all of this?

LIPPMANN: Well, I didn't say that the world was
going to go just the way we want it to go. What I say
is that as between our world, the Western world,
with us in a military sense in the center of it, and
the Communist world, the Soviet Union, the balance
is more in our favor than it was a year ago. Now,
what happens in Cuba and what happens in Brazil,
and so on, is going to go on for a century in one
form or another, and anybody who thinks that
out of a favorable turn in the balance of power
he's going to get Utopia, or the world just as he wants
it, doesn't understand the nature of things. When

history goes on — who won the modern age? It's gone on for five hundred years, changing. One power was up. Another power was down. You don't win ages. I mean, you can win a battle on the ground, but it's just foolish to talk about victory in a thing as large as the process of history on a global scale. I believe our society, while it is going to change from within, and is changing, is not going to be overwhelmed or buried, as Mr. Khrushchev once said, by this other society. If anything, I think our influence is growing, or has been growing in very recent times. It was going down. Now I think it's begun to go up. But I don't think we'd better be complacent about it. I'd keep my fingers crossed.

V

Lippmann and Charles Collingwood

The most extraordinary event preceding this broadcast was the confrontation of the Soviet Union by the United States on October 22, 1962, when President Kennedy revealed the existence of the Soviet missile sites in Cuba; six days later Nikita Khrushchev acceded to the President's demands that the weapons be removed, and the world breathed a sigh of relief. Relief was also felt when the troops which Red China had poised menacingly on the Indian border were withdrawn. In Europe, France vetoed Great Britain's somewhat tardy application to join the Common Market; and on the death of Hugh Gaitskell, Britain's Labour Party turned to Harold Wilson as its new leader. The continents were drawn closer together by the launching of the Telstar communications satellite. Two Soviet astronauts were launched into space in separate craft and after orbiting many times they landed three days later within a few minutes of one another. New hope for the brotherhood of man was expressed by Pope John XXIII in his opening of the Ecumenical Council, but not in Mississippi, where Governor Ross Barnett barred the admission of a Negro student, James Meredith, to the state university despite a Federal court order. The rioting which followed, in which two people were killed and seventy-five injured, set a sorry precedent for the Deep South.

May 1, 1963

COLLINGWOOD: In your broadcast a year ago, you suggested that the balance of power was moving in favor of the West. Do you still think that process is continuing?

LIPPMANN: No, I think the situation has become enormously more complicated during the past year, owing to the fact that both in East and West there is a breakup or disarray in the alliances; and therefore you can no longer compare simply the power of the West, which meant the power of the United States, with the power of the Soviet Union. They're no longer units. Moscow has lost control of Communism in Asia; and in the West, the movement toward unity which was very promising a year ago has been stopped, if not prevented, since General de Gaulle's famous press conference in January.

COLLINGWOOD: How deep does the split between Russia and China go?

LIPPMANN: Well, it goes very deep really. You spoke of Russia and China, and that's correct, because the split is deepest between Russia and China. The Soviet Union, or Russia, the whole movement of its population and its history is west to east, across

Siberia to the Pacific Ocean. The movement of the
Chinese — with their expanding population — is
northward, through Manchuria and Sinkiang, and
that causes a collision between these two. That issue, that conflict, has never yet been resolved peaceably and it is a fundamental conflict of interest between Russia and China. Now, besides that, both of
them are Communist states, and until this summer,
this year, China accepted the primacy of Russia in
the field of Communist ideology. That is broken down.
The Chinese are openly hostile to the Russians, and
all that happens in Asia around the enormous mass
of China, north from Korea around to India, is out of
Russian control.

COLLINGWOOD: Then you suggest that this is going to get worse rather than better, from Russia's
and China's point of view?

LIPPMANN: Yes. There's no evidence that the Russians will be able to control the Chinese. They may
slow them down, but they no longer are able to give
them orders. Now when the agreement was made in
Geneva in 1961 about Laos, the Russians were the
masters. There's no evidence — there's every reason
to think they're no longer the masters in Laos, that
the Chinese are the people who call the tune.

COLLINGWOOD: What can we do about their ex-
pansion in that direction?

LIPPMANN: Well, that thrust, I think, will have to be contained on the western side by finally working out a coalition between India and Pakistan; and on the eastern side, it will have to be contained mainly by American sea power, because I agree with General MacArthur, who told the Senate that we should not get involved in jungle wars in Asia. That will not cause the pressure of the Chinese movement to stop, but it'll narrow it and contain it, and we will be able to play for time while we build up the power of India and Pakistan.

COLLINGWOOD: But India and Pakistan are almost at war with each other.

LIPPMANN: Yes, but they've got to get at peace with one another. They can't afford to go on being at war with one another, because they're both threatened by this thing. India is threatened — attacked — her frontiers were attacked; and Pakistan is the next thing, because there's a whole large part of Pakistan which is right in the way of the Chinese. That's East Pakistan, which is, as you know, a thousand miles to the east of the rest of Pakistan, and that can only be defended by the Indians with the help that we can give them. If the Chinese ever break through there completely, Pakistan will be knocked to pieces in its eastern section.

COLLINGWOOD: Now, what effect is this conflict

between Russia and China having within Russia itself? Is Khrushchev's position really in danger?

LIPPMANN: Nobody can quite say whether his position is in danger, but his position is that of an aging statesman who is bound in the end — in some reasonable time — to give up at least some, if not all of his power. Nature is taking care of that, not the Chinese.

COLLINGWOOD: Is that the explanation for Khrushchev's testiness — his rages against the artists and the poets, which certainly can't be explained by a difference in aesthetic appreciation?

LIPPMANN: No, I don't think that's the explanation. I don't think, necessarily, just because he's getting older that he's getting more of an old fogey. I don't think that's the explanation. I think the explanation is that in Russia — it's always been true, and he knows this — that big revolutionary movements are preceded by artistic revolutions. It's the artists and intellectuals who are the first people who go in revolt; and with this kind of system that exists in the Soviet Union, if they give too much freedom the whole thing will fall apart. A Soviet system — a totalitarian system is always very fragile. It isn't tough and durable. On the other hand, they can't make the system work with totalitarianism, and I think that's where Khrushchev is irritable because he's, in a sense, stumped. He's in a blind alley, and he doesn't quite know how to get out of it. I don't think it's got anything to do with what we do, or what the Chinese do. It's in the nature of the Soviet system.

COLLINGWOOD: Well, now, are we able to exploit this difference within the Communist system?

LIPPMANN: No. As long as we could present the picture to the world of a growing unity within Europe, and between Europe and North America, and then both of them with Latin America, and so on, the magnetic attraction of this was enormous on all — all over the Soviet Empire, on Poland and Czechoslovakia — they want to join it too. Now, that is stopped for the moment. That's where things have changed in the past year, and so we are not — that's the only way we could exploit it, by offering a very attractive alternative.

COLLINGWOOD: Now this weakness then, on our side, this inability of the western coalition to preserve its unity, is a new factor?

LIPPMANN: The basis of it is that Europe has recovered from the war, and — you see, the situation, the relation between Europe and the United States during the war was really, in point of view of history, an extremely abnormal one. Europe depended entirely on the protection of the United States, and it also depended on the United States as its banker, as its financier. United States had all the gold and, with the atomic weapons, all the power at the end of the Second World War. Well, Europe has outgrown that. Europe is now a very prosperous part — Western Europe, I'm talking about — a very prosperous part of the world. Its rate of economic growth is greater than even ours. It has gold reserves which are growing. They're not as great as ours, but their liabilities are less, so that in a sense they're stronger.

Also, as time has passed, they no longer believe in what they had reason to believe in ten years ago, that they were about to be attacked by the Soviet Union. They don't think the Cold War is on to the degree that most Americans do. General de Gaulle would never dare to do what he's doing if he thought it were, because it's all right for him to talk about having an independent nuclear power, but he hasn't got it, and he isn't going to have it for perhaps ten years, and what's going to happen in these ten years? What General de Gaulle says is, "Nothing. The danger has passed." He couldn't do it if he thought it was a danger.

COLLINGWOOD: You suggested that the West is now entering a post-postwar period, as the leaders of the war and immediate postwar period fade into the shadows.

LIPPMANN: Well, the postwar period is ending, and as it usually happens about fifteen years after a great war, the settlement of that war begins to come undone, and a new era begins. The Napoleonic Wars and the Congress of Vienna — which ended in the Congress of Vienna in 1815 — were pretty well liquidated by 1830. Our Civil War was liquidated by 1880 — the Reconstruction Period. The First World War and the settlements of Versailles, made in 1918-1919, were finished with the rise of Hitler by 1933. We are now eighteen years from the end of the Second World War; we are in that same kind of change, and the reason for it is not very complicated. It is that the men who fought the war are fifteen years older, and the men who fought in the war but didn't command are fifteen years older too. It was symbolized, if you like, in the Inauguration of 1961, when outgoing President Eisenhower, who had been the Supreme Commander of all Western Forces, rode down Pennsylvania Avenue with the commander of a PT boat who was to be inaugurated. Now, that is the change that has occurred and is occurring in all countries in Europe. Adenauer is going. De Gaulle may have a few more years, but not many. Macmillan is going. The war generation is passing out, and the reason is perfectly simple. The young men grow up and the old men fade out and that's why the change takes place.

COLLINGWOOD: It's curious that General de Gaulle, who certainly is a figure of the past, is in a sense the instrument of — or one of the instruments of this change from postwar arrangements to the post-postwar arrangements.

LIPPMANN: That is true and it's quite characteristic of de Gaulle. De Gaulle's greatest quality is his vision. He has shown again and again that his capacity to see what the situation really is — not what people think it is, or are in the habit of saying it is — what it really is, and the direction in which it's going, is unequaled. He is the most prophetic mind of our generation. Somebody said of him — I think it was Jean Monnet — he's a great man of decision. He's able to say, "This is over, the postwar period is over. France is no longer under the tutelage of the United States" — but then he's not a man of action, so what he does after he's decided not to do something, is always vague. And de Gaulle saw that the postwar system and the institutions and NATO and all that are no longer necessary in the sense we thought they were necessary during the postwar period; but what comes after them — he has no real plan. And so Europe is drifting around while the changing of the guard and the elections take place. It will take another two or three years.

COLLINGWOOD: Does de Gaulle's opposition to it mean that the idea of a united interdependent Europe is finished for the time being?

LIPPMANN: All we can say about that is that he has stopped it, and we — we and the West Europeans, the Germans particularly, and the Italians too, but mainly the Germans — prevent him from realizing what he wants; so it's a stalemate.

COLLINGWOOD: His idea of the future more or less depends on the persistence of the special relationship between West Germany and France, doesn't it?

LIPPMANN: It does.

COLLINGWOOD: Do you think that will survive him and Adenauer?

LIPPMANN: No, it won't survive Adenauer. Adenauer's immediate successor now, we think, assuming that Adenauer doesn't change his mind, which he is capable of doing — Adenauer's successor is Erhard. Well, Erhard is an old-fashioned liberal — a Western liberal. He believes in trade and international trade and trading overseas and trading with Great Britain and North America and Asia, and so on. He doesn't believe in this rather tight nationalistic kind of Europe which de Gaulle's talking about. De Gaulle doesn't want him any more than Adenauer wants him.

COLLINGWOOD: Do you think that Adenauer would have been better advised if he had left the scene earlier and more gracefully than he's doing?

LIPPMANN: He had a wonderful way of ending his career. He should have become President instead of Chancellor of Germany, which he started to be, and then suddenly he looked at Erhard, I think, and decided that he wouldn't stand that, so he became Chancellor instead, and his last term as Chancellor, this term, has not been a happy one for him or for his reputation. They've had these dreadful scandals inside the administration. He isn't responsible for them, but they taint the administration. And I know that last autumn when they were having the big scandal over the so-called disclosure of military documents, I happened to be in Bonn, and they would have thrown him out then except they said, "He's too great a man. He's done too much for Germany. We're not going to let him end his life, his career on a disgrace. We're going to see him through this." And that's the only reason he's still Chancellor, I think.

COLLINGWOOD: How will history judge Adenauer?

As those Germans you were talking about judge him?

LIPPMANN: Oh, I think history will speak better of Adenauer than we can speak of him at this moment. He's the German who rescued Germany — restored — yes, rescued Germany from the demoralization and defeat and disgrace of the Nazi regime, and Germany has become respectable, a respectable member of world society, which it wasn't at the end of the war.

COLLINGWOOD: You've made it clear what the transition from the postwar world is *from*. What is it *to*? What kind of governments are going to emerge in the West?

LIPPMANN: Well, in the West, indications are that they are going to be center governments. The class struggle is fading out in advanced countries. It's faded out in this country, and it's fading out in Germany, Italy, certainly in Great Britain — and in France, it's harder to talk about it, because the thing is so obscured by General de Gaulle's domination of the scene. But that is essentially the movement, and this movement toward the center and away from the two extremes, is what's going to be in power in Europe in the next few years to come.

COLLINGWOOD: Is this same process of transition taking place in the Soviet Union?

LIPPMANN: No, they can't, not the same thing. The process that's taking place there, I think, is that they have a generation who didn't know Lenin, didn't know the Revolution, and who were the young men, the PT boat commanders, and so on, in the Second World War, and they are doing very well. Soviet economy is growing, and life is getting better. They are getting housing and clothing and food, and so on; but the thing is also getting more complicated. You can't sit in the Kremlin and run that thing as you could twenty years ago. There's too much of it. It's too big. And also, you can't have all the ideas in the Kremlin, and they are finding, which is just exactly what Western society found two hundred years ago, beginning about then, that if you are going to have an industrial society, you have to have liberty; and Khrushchev, in a way, has been fumbling around with this. He wants more liberty — in fact, he knows he has to have it, and yet he doesn't know how to do it. I think that's where they are.

COLLINGWOOD: In a sense, then, the Russians are becoming more like us.

LIPPMANN: Yes, and less like the Chinese.

COLLINGWOOD: There seems to be some sort of mutual restraint operating between the United States and Russia — you have seen it in Berlin and Cuba. How long do you think that will last?

LIPPMANN: Well, I think the restraint — when you say restraint you mean we hesitate, we don't do the things that we think might lead to nuclear war.

COLLINGWOOD: I suppose that's what I mean.

LIPPMANN: That is what restraint is.

COLLINGWOOD: Yes.

LIPPMANN: Well, I think that's going to last as long as the danger of nuclear war, unless we go crazy. You never can count on what would happen if we all went crazy, but assuming we don't, and we haven't yet, and although we've been in some very tight squeezes, as it were, in Cuba last October, we are going to stop just short of what we think, with our best judgment, is the point at which there will be war. That is the essence of the Cuban problem.

COLLINGWOOD: What brought the Russians to Cuba, and why are they still there?

LIPPMANN: Well, the thing that brought them there was the fact that Castro proclaimed himself a Communist, and we had helped the first attempt at an invasion in 1961, the Bay of Pigs, and as a Communist he appealed for help, and they couldn't disown him. That's one part of it. The other part is, and may have been more important — it probably accounts for the missiles. The Soviet Union is behind the United States in nuclear weapons. We're the superior power, and if they could have landed and set up forty or so medium-range missiles, they would have had a first-strike capacity against the continental United States, as well as the Panama Canal and the whole Caribbean, which would have changed the balance of power in their favor. They were a little bit like a team in a football game, throwing a forward pass in the hope of getting a touchdown before the game ends; and that was stopped, of course, and now they're there because there is no way out of there. They can't withdraw without taking a terrible defeat, and also they don't want Castro to collapse.

COLLINGWOOD: What can we do about it? Do we just have to let them sit there?

LIPPMANN: I tell you, we have to make up our minds whether we are in such a hurry to get those Russian troops out of there that we are willing to risk war, go to war, or whether we're not. If Castro were a mortal threat to the United States, we'd have to risk a mortal war, but he isn't. He injures our pride — he's an affront to our pride. He's an awful nuisance. He's an annoyance. He's a mischief-maker. He does do propaganda. His example is bad, but he isn't threatening to conquer or destroy the United States, and you can't risk the destruction of the world — because it would come to that if it were a nuclear war — destruction of the Northern Hemisphere, just because you don't like this man and find him an awful nuisance. You only go to war — modern war — for the absolutely ultimate reasons. You can't do it for a lesser reason.

Now if we're not going to go to war, then we can only use measures which are generally described as short of war, which is what we are doing. We have embargo, we are surveying them. We are patrolling them. We are squeezing them, isolating them, cutting off their connections, reducing their trade, forcing them into dependence on us. That's all — those are all just short of war, and of course, if Cuba were a big power, they'd be at war with us long ago over what we've already done to Cuba. But they're not, and the Russians say, "You keep quiet, don't go beyond this," because they don't want to go to war either. Now, I think everybody — I'll come to the one or two exceptions in a second — who has studied the problem critically, notably, for example, Senator Keating of New York, has reached an agreement with the administration that war is unacceptable. They are not going to go to war. There is nothing that happened in Cuba yet that is so dangerous to the United States that we can afford to burn up the world over it, if necessary.

Senator Keating and President Kennedy and I think everybody, except maybe Senator Goldwater,

is against invasion; well, Senator Goldwater is
against invasion; nobody wants to invade Cuba. I
don't know of anybody that says he wants to. Nobody
wants to blockade Cuba, because if you blockade
Cuba, you've got either to capture or sink Russian
ships. That's the only point of blockade. There are
no other ships that matter in there.

Now, there are people like Mr. Nixon and Governor Rockefeller, and Senator Goldwater, who say,
"Why, we must do more," and when you look at it
very closely, and ask, "What more? Do you want
war?" "No," they say, "we don't really — we don't
want to — we don't have to go to war." "Well, then,
what do you want to do?" Well, what they really
want to do is threaten war, and the theory is that in
October the President threatened Khrushchev with
war if he didn't withdraw the offensive missiles and
he did withdraw them; therefore, if we said to him,
"Get out of Cuba — take your troops away. Let Castro fall," he would do the same. Well, nobody knows
that, and the President of the United States has to
make up his mind. In October, the presence of forty
missiles with possible nuclear warheads was a very
great actual threat to the United States. Seventeen
thousand Russian troops, if that's the right number,
with tanks in Cuba are not a threat to the United

States. They cannot cross the ninety miles of water. They have nothing but launches and motorboats to do it. They are not capable; whereas the missiles were. So the President took the terrible risk on the missiles, but he can't take that risk over just the fact that the Russians are there, and the only difference of opinion, really, among people who stop to analyze it in this country is between those who think you could bluff Khrushchev into surrendering, and those who don't think that you can bluff him that far. That's the difference of opinion.

COLLINGWOOD: And you feel that the risk involved in the bluff is not worth the possible profit?

LIPPMANN: You can't gamble that way with the lives of masses of mankind.

COLLINGWOOD: Will the Cubans take care of Castro and his Russian friends — without our help?

LIPPMANN: I cannot prophesy. I don't know. We hope so, but we can't guarantee it. And I think we might as well be prepared. If we are going to stick to measures short of war — in other words, if we're not going to give an ultimatum to the Russians and say, "Get out, or else we'll invade Cuba and blockade it," if we're not going to do that, then we may not be able to solve the Cuban problem until we've solved the other problems of conflict. In other words, until there is, if there ever will be, a general settlement with the Soviet Union. I mean, Cuba and Berlin and Vietnam may all be one bag.

COLLINGWOOD: That we must live with until a general arrangement in the world?

LIPPMANN: Yes, and we can live with it.

COLLINGWOOD: How are we going to stop the spread of infection from Castro's Cuba to the rest of Latin America?

LIPPMANN: You throw off infection by being healthy, and South America is not healthy. Again and again, in most countries, you have a problem of poverty and riches, of backwardness, of illiteracy, which has to be cured. Now, what we're trying to do in South America may not succeed, because it's something that is really unheard of in human history. We're trying to help a whole continent do what would be accomplished, or supposedly be accomplished, by a big revolution without having the revolution. That's what the Alliance for Progress is. They're to go on being peaceful, democratic and progressive, and their reactionary, or highly conservative people, who are against the measures of progress, are supposed gently to listen to reason and fold up. Now, I have my fingers crossed as to whether that's going to happen, and I think anybody who takes too rosy a view of the future of the Alliance for Progress in South America is whistling in the dark, if I may use a mixed metaphor.

COLLINGWOOD: Mr. Lippmann, you've dwelt on the postwar transition to a new era in Europe. In this country, President Kennedy may be the visible herald of a new generation in politics, but he hasn't been very successful in his innovations so far, has he?

LIPPMANN: Well, he hasn't been able to get many of the big measures of his program. He hasn't been nearly so successful as he thought he was going to be when he was running for President in 1960 and that most people thought he would be. Now, there are several reasons why he hasn't been. The first is, he won by a very narrow majority. The second is that although he was elected on major issues, I think it's fair to say that the bulk of public opinion really agrees with General Eisenhower. He's been dealing not merely with a Congress that doesn't agree with a great deal of his measures, but really with the American public that doesn't.

COLLINGWOOD: What is there in American public opinion that makes it difficult for him to convince them of his program?

LIPPMANN: The main thing is that the country is really very well off; in spite of the fact that our rate of economic growth is low, low compared with any advanced country in the world except Great Britain, this country is very prosperous indeed. But while there are unemployed, the hard truth of the matter is that the unemployed are politically not very powerful people, and although they're very important, all these people, they're not powerful enough to make any great impression on Congress or the general public.

COLLINGWOOD: You feel then that there isn't much more that the President could have done to further his program?

LIPPMANN: I think there are several things that I wish he had done, and I think he's been too cautious on measures to stimulate economic growth, because we are producing considerably below our capacity to produce. We are losing annually, in gross national product, perhaps thirty to thirty-five billion dollars, and the revenues from that would make a great difference both to the Federal budget and to the state and municipal budgets. Now he hasn't done that because the country really agrees with General Eisenhower that deficits are always bad; although General Eisenhower had the biggest one yet himself, they're always bad. Deficits are bad if they're permanent, but deficits over a business cycle of four or five years, and deficits in the time when the cycle is down, are good; and a lot of what is called spending and deficit is actually called by private business, investment. The Federal Government keeps its books in such a way that no matter what it buys, whether it hires an errand boy or builds a power dam, it's all the same; it's all spending. Nobody thinks it's a bad thing when the United States Steel Corporation or General Motors invests in and builds a new plant and borrows the money; that's considered development. But it always seems much worse if the government does it.

COLLINGWOOD: The President has been criticized as being more concerned with the process of politics than the results — with his image than with the substance. Do you feel there is any merit in those criticisms?

LIPPMANN: Well, I think, yes — I think there's some merit in it. He believes that measures have to be worked through by arrangements with Congress. He does not ever want to force measures as some leaders do — as the two Roosevelts did, as Wilson did. He is a man who works it out politically. He's one of them. He's one of the boys. That's his method of dealing politically. And that is a good thing and a bad thing. It has its good side and bad side. He's sometimes too cautious. I think he's been too cautious about the tax cut, for example. On the other hand, he's right, I think, not to get in a deadly fight over some other measures where there's no hope of doing anything except splitting the two ends of Pennsylvania Avenue from each other. Now you asked me about his image of himself, or something of that sort?

COLLINGWOOD: Yes.

LIPPMANN: He has a weakness. I think it's one of his serious — one of his two or three serious weaknesses as a public leader is that he does not want to be unpopular anywhere — anywhere — with anyone; and I think that a public leader, at times, has to get into struggles where somebody gets a bloody nose, and Kennedy doesn't want that ever; and that's where he differs from all his most successful predecessors who've been political leaders. All the others, the Roosevelts, and even Truman, and so on, they've always at some point got into a real struggle, and he doesn't — he avoids that.

COLLINGWOOD: The administration, as a whole, seems very conscious of its image. Besides the security angle, that must be partly what is behind the controversy over managed news.

LIPPMANN: Well, that is a silly controversy, and it all started from a very foolish remark made by the Secretary for Information in the Defense Department. All news given out by government is more or less managed. It always has been and always will be, but what you never do admit to the public is what Mr. Sylvester admitted: that he did it. That is the one mistake you're not allowed to make in this business. Under President Eisenhower the news was managed constantly and continually by Mr. Hagerty, who is really the biggest expert at it there is. The country didn't know how sick the President was when he had a heart attack. They thought he was still functioning as President when he wasn't. The government was being run by committee. The news was perfectly managed. Well, that's inevitable; and it's very naïve, it's very innocent to pretend that news isn't managed, and to talk as if there were such a thing as one absolutely perfect true version of the facts and that's the only fact — there is no such thing. All the news gets managed by the White House, by the Defense Department, by the managing editor, by the correspondent, by the columnist, by everybody.

COLLINGWOOD: Would you say that the President's performance so far has lived up to his own expectations of what he would like to have done?

LIPPMANN: No, I don't doubt he's disappointed. You see, it isn't that he has himself not done well. I don't think that's where the disappointment lies. First, he's disappointed in discovering that the country's opinion is not with him to the extent that he needs it with him if he's going to carry out his domestic program. In the second place, he's undoubtedly disappointed in discovering that the great structure of his foreign policy — which was to be, you know, Common Market in Europe, Britain joining it, both of them joining with the Atlantic community and the United States — has been brought to a halt, if it hasn't been broken down. Those are very disappointing results. Also, I would add a third disappointment. He thought he was going to deal with Khrushchev about the future of Communism, and now he's no longer able to deal with Khrushchev even if Khrushchev wanted to, because the Chinese are out of hand.

COLLINGWOOD: Mr. Lippmann, is the administration breaking any new ground in the arts and practices of government?

LIPPMANN: Yes, I think you could name some specific things that would be new ground. I think, for example, that in this administration the first really effective effort has been made to bring the military establishment, which is perfectly enormous, under civilian control. Now one can argue a lot about Secretary McNamara's judgment about whether the Boeing plane was better than the General Dynamics plane — whether he was right or wrong about that

— but never since the establishment was put together has any civilian control been as effective as his, and if he's wrong about how he exercises control, get a new Secretary — although I don't think we will get a better one, or one nearly so good — but let us keep our minds on the fact that control is at last being exercised.

COLLINGWOOD: What are the qualities in Secretary McNamara that have made him successful in controlling the military?

LIPPMANN: First of all, he's got an absolutely first-class mind. There's nobody who knows more about what he's talking about than he does. Up to now, almost always — there have been maybe some exceptions — the admirals and the generals knew more about the equipment than the civilian, and he bowed to them. That is no longer true. McNamara is quite capable of debating anywhere with any of these generals and admirals about the value of these planes. In fact, his whole argument, as far as I can make out, with the McClellan Committee is whether they will give him a chance to argue it. They're putting off the examination of McNamara.

COLLINGWOOD: The Secretary of Defense presides over the spending of a very considerable proportion of the national budget and the gross national product.

LIPPMANN: Ten per cent of all the wealth of the United States is disbursed by the Defense Department.

COLLINGWOOD: Do you think that's a healthy thing for our economy?

LIPPMANN: It's an unhealthy thing, but it's an unavoidable thing. We have to have this defense for all the reasons that everybody knows about the situation in the world, but we must never forget that it's a very, very dangerous and significant thing that so much of the money of the country, and so much of the brains, research, and resource of the country, is devoted to military purposes, and is under military command. And we must never take it for granted. We must have it, but we must always have it with the knowledge that this is something we have to keep watching.

COLLINGWOOD: The question then arises that if we didn't have it, would the money be spent for anything else? In his press conference last week, when the President was talking about the moon program, he said if we were to save money on this, it was not his judgment that it would be spent for education or housing or other things.

LIPPMANN: Well, I think he was being discouraged about Congress. I think he thought Congress doesn't want to spend money on anything except

military affairs. So if they didn't have to spend on
military affairs, they wouldn't spend it. But I think
the country has a lot of things it ought to spend
money on besides military things. I would put as the
highest priority a measure which is practically
stranded now, namely, Federal aid to education, because while you can wait a few years whether you
rebuild a slum, or whether you build a highway, that
can wait — you can do it later, if necessary — you
can't wait with the education of children. If you
don't educate them, they'll be uneducated when they
grow up, and they'll be the parents, uneducated
parents, of children who will be still less educated.
So you get a thing that is a vicious circle — vicious
spiral downward; and therefore, you can't let the
thing drift, and our education is quite inadequate.
And — now, you know why it's stalled. There's this
quarrel — conflict over whether aid to education
shall include the church schools, and particularly
the parochial schools, and that has got to be resolved.

COLLINGWOOD: How can it be resolved?

LIPPMANN: It is not beyond the wit of man, if he
means it, for us to find a way of aiding education,
whether it's in public schools or parochial schools,
without getting involved in the question of the teaching of religion.

COLLINGWOOD: Do you feel that concessions should be made to the parochial schools?

LIPPMANN: Yes, I do. We have to remember that we have laws in this country that every child must be educated, so we take that responsibility. We allow five million of them, or thereabouts — I think that's the figure — to be educated in these parochial schools. They are part of the American system of education. Otherwise, why do we allow them to be educated in these schools? If they're going to be educated in them, they should be educated as well as possible; therefore, if they need money, as private schools do, for textbooks, or laboratories, or even buildings, I think a way should be found of getting rid of this religious knot that we've tied ourselves into over that.

COLLINGWOOD: Are you implying that Federal aid to education is so important that you would be willing to break with tradition and see aid to parochial schools?

LIPPMANN: I am. I think it's so important that we cannot afford to postpone the improvement of education any longer.

COLLINGWOOD: Next year, 1964, is going to be an election year. The Democrats don't have any particular problem. Kennedy will undoubtedly be the nominee. But what are the Republicans' prospects?

LIPPMANN: You mean their chances of nominating someone, or of electing someone?

COLLINGWOOD: Of electing someone.

LIPPMANN: Well, they're in a very difficult position, assuming that the country remains as prosperous as it is today, and that there's no catastrophe abroad. But assuming that, and you have to make some assumption, their only hope is to be able to convince the country that they can do substantially what Kennedy is trying to do, only do it better. There isn't any other ground. They can't say we're against doing it, because that is the great center position where the mass of the votes lie, and Kennedy, quite rightly, has occupied that center. And Rockefeller really wants to occupy it too, and he believes the same thing. There's no difference in basic economic doctrine or philosophy between Kennedy and Rockefeller. The Rockefeller Reports on the economy and growth and deficits and budgets and education are identical, except for the changes of dates and updating figures, and so on, with the Kennedy program. And Rockefeller's difficulty is that he wants to agree with Kennedy in order to get the votes, and he wants to disagree with him in order to get nominated. And it's very difficult. I think he's in trouble, and although he looks like the front runner, I wouldn't be too surprised to see the Republicans nominate Romney,

who's more like the kind of man they're used to
nominating — if you look back thirty, forty years —
somebody who is not quite a Republican, and not
quite a Democrat. They haven't had an authentic
Republican since Warren Harding after the First
World War. I mean, Hoover was a Democrat before
he was — well, he worked for the Democratic administration. The Democrats tried to nominate him
before the Republicans did. Willkie, in 1940, was a
Democrat till a few weeks before he became a Republican candidate. General Eisenhower was almost
nominated in the Democratic Convention four years
before he was nominated in the Republican Convention.

COLLINGWOOD: Is this because, once again, of
the pull to the center that both parties have to face?

LIPPMANN: Yes, the pull to the center is very
strong in this country. We don't have a class struggle. The middle class in the United States includes
most of the working class, not all of it, but most of it.
And there is no very — we have no aristocratic feudal class on the other side. So most of this country is
middle class, and that's the center.

COLLINGWOOD: Where does that leave Senator
Goldwater, who certainly is a Republican?

LIPPMANN: Well, Senator Goldwater is the man;
if you wanted to make American politics logical and

clear and get a final clear-cut decision, the Republicans ought to nominate Goldwater and at last get a Republican who is a Republican. Now, whether they have got the nerve to do that, I don't know.

COLLINGWOOD: Are you implying that you're in the market for a Goldwater for President button, or do you mean that this would be an interesting test of the basic strength of the two parties?

LIPPMANN: Well, I'd like to see the issue put to the test once. We have been hearing for a generation that the Republican candidate is never a real Republican, and that's why he doesn't get elected; that he's always a "me too" man. Well, now, there's a man who is not a "me too" man, and I think it would be just as well to try it out once and let Kennedy and Goldwater, who is supposed to be a true Republican, fight it out and see what the country wants. They might as well get something out of their system which they need to get out of their system.

COLLINGWOOD: You say that Senator Goldwater is a real Republican. Do you think he's a real conservative?

LIPPMANN: No, I consider Kennedy a conservative. I consider Rockefeller a conservative. A conservative is not a man who wants to repeal everything that's happened in the last twenty years, but a man who wants to conserve it and make it grow, and have it develop, and the idea that a man cannot be liberal and progressive, can be liberal and not conservative, is a mistake. Good conservatives are liberal about how the laws are executed, and they're progressive about adapting them to changing conditions, and the idea that one man's a conservative but not liberal, and another man is liberal but not conservative, is just misunderstanding of terms.

COLLINGWOOD: Mr. Lippmann, looking back on our conversation in this past hour, it seems to me that you have counseled for the United States a policy of patience and fortitude. Do you really think that that is the appropriate posture for the nation with the greatest power that any nation has had in the history of the world?

LIPPMANN: Yes, I do, and I think it was Aristotle who said that the finest attribute of power is restraint, and that there's nothing so impressive as to have great power and to use it magnanimously, patiently, and with restraint. That's exactly what the greatest power ought to be. It cannot go off on adventures. It can't go off on binges of popular emotion. It has to be conscious of the fact that the safety of all mankind, in one sense, is in its hands; and that's such a responsibility that it can't be exercised intemperately — jingoistically — incautiously.

COLLINGWOOD: It could be said that we have

been acting with restraint ever since we had exclusive possession of nuclear force, and that this has not noticeably ameliorated the conditions of the world in which we live.

LIPPMANN: Well, it would be wrongly argued if it were. Because in that time Europe, which was prostrated and demoralized and helpless, has become a great power, and the recovery of Europe, and with it the dependencies of Europe, is one of the great accomplishments of a postwar era. What more could we possibly want than to see it reviving? And that has been done because we've had strength but also patience. If we'd upset the apple cart and turned the whole thing into a blazing mass of rubble, what would Europe be like today? An awful lot of people in this country want all the results of winning a war without the pains of fighting it, and that causes an awful lot of confusion. They want to get all the results that would come from destroying Russia, but they don't want to take the risks of destroying Russia, because they don't know how well we would be treated, what would happen to us. And you can't have it that way. You have to be grown up and live in a world where you can use power up to a point, but not beyond that.

VI

Lippmann and Eric Sevareid

This was a time when violence was on the rampage. The world was shocked by the assassination of President Kennedy, and this, the murder of the assassin, and pictures of the police brutality employed against the Negroes in Birmingham had damaged the American reputation abroad. In August, before the death of President Kennedy, the United States, Britain, and the Soviet Union had signed the partial nuclear test ban treaty in Geneva; Pope John XXIII had died; Harold Macmillan and Konrad Adenauer had retired as heads of their respective governments; Ngo Dinh Diem's regime in South Vietnam had been overthrown; Khrushchev had his first open break with China; and the crisis in Cyprus had reached the boiling point.

April 8, 1964

SEVAREID: Mr. Lippmann, you have been writing and with great influence for some fifty years about the affairs of this country. I can't think of any record to match it in American journalism — not even Horace Greeley's. You have been personally acquainted, and are, with Presidents, Cabinet officers, military people, many people of high rank. In fact, Presidents have come to see you. How do you maintain a relationship with them that is intimate enough so that you can go to them when you want information and yet write critically about them if necessary? Do you restrain yourself in any fashion to keep that relationship?

LIPPMANN: No, I think there are certain rules of hygiene in the relationship between a newspaper correspondent and high officials — people in authority — which are very important and which one has to observe. Newspapermen cannot be the cronies of great men. Once a man — even if you have known him more or less as a crony for years and he becomes something like a governor — much less a President — it's all over. You can't call him by first name anymore. I've known several Presidents whom I knew by their first names long before they were President, and I would never think of calling them by them when they got into the White House. I think it is advantageous for the President to be able to talk to somebody who won't exploit him, or betray him, or talk his mind; and it's certainly an advantage to the correspondent to know what's really going on so he won't make a fool of himself. But there always has to be a certain distance between high public officials and newspapermen. I wouldn't say a wall or a fence, but an air space, that's very necessary.

SEVAREID: You must be free to be critical of a given individual —

LIPPMANN: You've got to accustom them to it. Now, I must say, lots of them don't get accustomed to it.

SEVAREID: You mean the officials or the reporters?

LIPPMANN: Officials. I mean a lot of them are very, very friendly to you until someday you say something they don't like, and then the friendship cools. I'm not speaking of any particular individual, but I have had that experience more than once in my life.

SEVAREID: Well, this is particularly interesting to me, because a number of opinion-makers, as they are called, have been promoted because of their supposed intimacy with men in very high positions. Is this a bad method of operation — a bad relationship?

LIPPMANN: I don't want to criticize what others do, but I don't think it's a good principle to advance your career or tie yourself up with a candidate in the hope that you'll then be the inside fellow. I think that's bad journalism.

SEVAREID: Is there a lot of that in Washington now?

LIPPMANN: [Waves hand without comment, suggesting that there is]

SEVAREID: Well, to go to something more impersonal and more important, Mr. Lippmann, a couple of years ago you said that we were achieving a superior position in terms of power in the world, vis-à-vis the Russians, and a year ago you felt that our alliance was coming somewhat unstuck. How do you feel about this general balance now?

LIPPMANN: I think that we're living in the aftermath of the threat of nuclear war between the Soviet Union and the United States. And that threat has for the time being been dissipated as a result of the fact that the United States achieved superiority in nuclear weapons, but of course not omnipotence. In other words, we're in no danger of a threat — of an attack — by the Soviet Union; on the other hand, we're in no position to order the Soviet Union around. This stalemate with our own superiority was demonstrated in the Cuban crisis and is, I think, enshrined in the test ban treaty. The test ban treaty is really, if you look at it from here, an acceptance by Russia of our existing superiority, and an admission that while we are superior, they can live with it. We can't use it as a threat to their existence.

SEVAREID: Well, now, what is the result of all this in world politics? Are the great powers paralyzed by this thing?

LIPPMANN: The result of it is that the military alliances and military arrangements — and I'm not talking only of NATO but of the alliances in Asia — which were based on the fact that the world had only two powers, and that they might go to war, are now coming apart. You see, when you had the terribly dangerous confrontation of these two nuclear powers, everybody was so frightened that they crowded into one camp or the other. Once that fear has been lifted, they begin to tend to their own ambitions and troubles, and so on. That's why the world is much more disorderly, yet much less dangerous.

SEVAREID: Are you then less disturbed because of all this by reason of what has been happening with the North Atlantic Alliance?

LIPPMANN: Yes, I agree with General de Gaulle.

The Alliance — if you mean by the Alliance, the agreement — this very solemn agreement that if one of us is attacked we will all go to the help — that is not coming apart. What is coming apart is the military structure of the integrated forces that General Eisenhower originally commanded as Supreme Commander and which is called the NATO establishment. That, General de Gaulle believes, is obsolete because there is no danger of a European collapse — it was devised to prevent a Soviet or Red Army invasion of Western Europe.

SEVAREID: Then it succeeded?

LIPPMANN: It succeeded, and it's outlived the necessity for it, and that's why the Europeans no longer really give it any great support.

SEVAREID: Well, this depolarization of the world, so-called, what is it going to mean in other terms?

LIPPMANN: Europe is recovering, of course. It has recovered economically, in Western Europe, remarkably. In fact, it's entirely recovered, you might say. But Europe, as a whole, is still split down the middle, and the full recovery of Europe won't have taken place until that fissure is over; in other words, until Germany is reunified and Eastern Europe becomes part of a larger European community.

SEVAREID: Is that happening in small ways?

LIPPMANN: Yes, there's a great deal of evidence

to show that it is happening. For instance, the Western Germans — the Bonn Republic — are now entered into relations which are formal in everything but name with the Eastern countries — Poland and Hungary, and so on. The trade economic ties between Western Germany and Eastern Europe are growing very rapidly — more rapidly than any other — and the old day of absolute division is over.

SEVAREID: Mr. Khrushchev has just talked about a good dish of goulash as better than revolution. Does this mean in your mind a fundamental change in the Russian pattern of approaching the world?

LIPPMANN: Basically, yes. Marxism is a dying creed in Russia. No, Mr. Khrushchev wouldn't admit that but it's a dying creed because it doesn't fit the kind of industrialized modern economy that the Soviets have begun to develop.

SEVAREID: Well, Russia's become as far as Communism goes, the "established church," in a sense, with China the "church militant."

LIPPMANN: Yes.

SEVAREID: Is this change really good for our interests? How serious a matter is China for us?

LIPPMANN: Well, she's not nearly so serious as Russia was five years ago, because she is not a nuclear power, and therefore she's not capable of the kind of thing that Russia was capable of.

SEVAREID: You don't feel very concerned about what China is trying to do?

LIPPMANN: I feel very much concerned about her influence, but it can't be done by sheer nuclear force. She doesn't have it. And I think China can be contained peaceably for another ten or fifteen years, and then she will be very much like the Soviet Union today.

SEVAREID: You sound as though we have very little to worry about, then. You're not worried about what may happen in Southeast Asia?

LIPPMANN: Yes, I think we have in Southeast Asia — we have a very serious thing there for which it's hard to see any satisfactory solution.

SEVAREID: President Kennedy said he did believe in the "domino theory," that if one part of Southeast Asia falls, the rest will go. Do you believe in that?

LIPPMANN: Well, I don't think it's all going to go like dominoes. I mean, if the worst happened in Vietnam — and I might say what I think is the worst that could happen to us. It would be the overthrow of the government by Vietnamese — South Vietnamese, who would then proceed to negotiate what would amount to a surrender to North Vietnam, and one of the terms would be the order for us to leave the country. We would lose our influence in the whole of Southeast Asia, which includes the Southeast Asia peninsula and Indonesia. And loss of influence for a great power is a very serious thing.

SEVAREID: How do we explain to people why the United States is involved in that war? Ought we be in it?

LIPPMANN: Well, I tell you: there was a vacuum. The old empires, the British Empire, the French Empire, the Dutch Empire broke down. They were conquered by the Japanese and then the Japanese Empire broke down. There was no government, and we were involved in all these places. And we allowed ourselves, and maybe we had to — there are some differences of opinion about that — to get sucked into Vietnam when the French left. I believe in the old-fashioned American strategic doctrine which was in force before Korea — never to get engaged in a land war on the mainland of Asia. Sea power, air power, yes, but never land. And I've heard it said by a very eminent American soldier that any American who committed American troops to a land war in Asia should have his head examined. That's the prejudice with which I approach this thing, and I would never have gotten in as deeply as we did get into Vietnam, but we're in, and you can't cry over spilled milk. The question is, how do you finish with it.

SEVAREID: Is General de Gaulle and his proclamations about that helping us or harming us now?

LIPPMANN: It's very difficult to say. The proclamations don't make a great deal of difference to us. We have had a government in Saigon which was corrupt and reactionary — the Diem government — and which we did our best to hope would disappear, which it did. That government was probably getting ready to negotiate some kind of an arrangement with North Vietnam. It certainly wasn't fighting the war very vigorously in South Vietnam.

SEVAREID: Do you really feel it's possible to negotiate some neutral status for that country?

LIPPMANN: I don't know — it may be too late. I think it has been possible, and I think the French — from what I know of them — wonder whether it isn't too late. But if anything is negotiated that does make a settlement there short of the actual military conquest of Indochina by the Chinese, it'll have to be done with China. And General de Gaulle, at least, has analyzed it correctly. Whether he can still pull it off, I don't know.

SEVAREID: There are a number of people who call him a mischief-maker and say he's broken up all the grand designs for the postwar world in Europe, in relation to us, and now in his recognizing of China. Is this mischief for us, really?

LIPPMANN: Well, of course, if you have a frozen

position and somebody breaks out of that and does things that don't accept the assumptions that you've accepted, that always seems mischievous and it's a nuisance. All our plans get thrown into confusion, but we have to open our minds to the possibility that on a lot of these things he may be right, and we may be wrong.

SEVAREID: By saying that certain things are the real realities, he may be bringing them about.

LIPPMANN: Well, take an example from Southeast Asia. He may be right that it's impossible to stabilize Southeast Asia without coming to terms with China. Now, we may not be able to do that. I know we can't because we have commitments to the Nationalists and Chiang Kai-shek, but de Gaulle doesn't have those commitments, and he's able to do it. And therefore the fact that he doesn't do what he would have to do in the period when we were omnipotent — practically — in the world, should not disturb us.

SEVAREID: Can he do these things because he personally is a very powerful figure even if his country is essentially weak in relation to us? He is not picking up the responsibility in these places.

LIPPMANN: Yes, he is. Only he doesn't think, for instance, of a place like Southeast Asia — he knows from nine years' warfare that the French conducted there that you cannot get a military solution of Southeast Asia.

SEVAREID: But if there were a neutrality agreement, still it would be American power, not French, that would have to guarantee it.

LIPPMANN: Certainly, certainly, and he'd be the first, I think, to admit that. But it won't be done by American power, by our bombers and advisers flying around in helicopters in South Vietnam. That's a necessary thing; I don't wish to be misunderstood. We have to try and stabilize a government before we can do anything else; but the great power that we have is economic, and the sea and air power. That's our power in Southeast Asia. Otherwise it's way beyond our reach.

SEVAREID: Again about General de Gaulle, Mr. Lippmann, doesn't he too suffer from what Senator Fulbright called mythology?

LIPPMANN: Well, I don't doubt that everybody has his myths, and he undoubtedly has his, which is about the grandeur of France. But the positive side of de Gaulle — the thing that will make him regarded, I think, as a genius in history — is his ability to foresee what is happening now and in the near future. And he's the first head of state who has realized and acted upon the realization that the postwar period had ended. That's the meaning of de Gaulle in Europe.

SEVAREID: Do you agree with his prophecies about Russia and her gradual move back into the Western world?

LIPPMANN: Yes, I think that's happening and the Russians are very conscious of it; and in Eastern Europe — where I was not long ago, in Hungary and Poland — the interest in being Western is very extraordinary.

SEVAREID: Would you say then, Mr. Lippmann, that the Cold War in relation to Russia, if not China, is really over?

LIPPMANN: The Cold War in its dangerous and malignant phase, which was when the race for the nuclear weapons was the ultimate thing — that's over. The rivalry of the political systems — the social systems — is not over, and probably won't be over for a generation.

SEVAREID: Well, the world has changed. Maybe our policies and thinking about it haven't changed that rapidly, but aren't we really overextended in too many ways and in too many places? Would we be wiser if we concentrated our foreign aid efforts in fewer places?

LIPPMANN: Yes, I think so. You see, we have

used foreign aid — that's why the thing is really, in a sense, very unpopular with the Congress — we've used it — it's an awful description — as a kind of "slush fund" around the periphery of Asia. I mean, we support armies, give them arms they don't need, we give them planes they don't know how to fly, just to keep the officer class happy because they're the people who control the government and they threaten that if we don't subsidize them, they'll go over and join the Communists. Now, that part of it I think we have to do. Every big government has a "slush fund." There's no use fooling yourself about that, and we mustn't be too moralistic or serious. But genuine foreign aid of the kind which is really intended to develop an underdeveloped country should be concentrated in those places where there's some chance of success.

SEVAREID: We are not deeply involved in Africa yet. We are in Latin America, we are in Asia. Is the trend now to try to pull back, or ought we be further into Africa?

LIPPMANN: I think the trend is to limit our commitments abroad rather than to extend them. And Africa, I would say, Africa south of the Sahara, is a place where we should never get in and be the primary power. For a number of reasons, partly because we are overcommitted and partly because we ourselves have an African problem in this country, we are not well suited to take a leading part in Africa south of the Sahara. So I think we should always be the second man, or third man, not the first man in those issues.

SEVAREID: Mr. Lippmann, is Cyprus the kind of place where this country ought to be involved?

LIPPMANN: Well, this country has to be involved, but not actively, and it isn't actively involved insofar as we have no troops there. I think that's a good example of how we should proceed in places where we don't want to get directly involved, namely, through the United Nations, or through some other alliance. But we are not in the front of the thing. We're not responsible for who gets killed and who doesn't get killed in a Cypriot village.

SEVAREID: Are we learning a little sense of reticence now?

LIPPMANN: Yes, there are increasing signs of it. I think we're increasingly realizing that we are not, as we were apparently at the end of the Second World War, omnipotent. We had everything — everybody was prostrate but the United States. We had the only nuclear weapons there were. We had all the money that there was disposable, that could be lent to anybody. Russia was prostrate; all of Europe was prostrate. Eastern Europe didn't exist. China was in terrible condition. Japan was prostrate. From that we developed an illusion that this omnipotence would last forever, and the great thing we're having to learn now — have had to begin to learn in the past three or four or five years — is that that period is over. That's what's meant by the postwar ending.

SEVAREID: Well, is this what you take Senator Fulbright to mean when he talks about the persistence of a mythology in our thinking about the world?

LIPPMANN: Yes. When he's speaking about myths persisting, he means what we believed — and what was probably true when we believed it, ten, fifteen years — well, back to the Second World War — about Russia, about China, about various countries. And the conceptions of what these countries are like and what they're up to stay frozen while actually events move on, and that's what he's talking about.

SEVAREID: But how do you unfreeze the given practical position we have, our problem on Cuba, for example. What can be done?

LIPPMANN: Well, I don't think we're doing badly about Cuba. The Russian-Soviet people are withdrawing. They are down to very few people now, and all the military people will be gone in a few months. In fact, there's a little subsidiary worry in our minds, now that they've left and are not manning the anti-aircraft guns, that they're in the hands of Castro, which may be more dangerous than when the Russians were there. However, we'll get by that. This is not a problem which will have a quick solution. If it has a peaceful and satisfactory solution over a number of years, that's good enough for us. And I think that the time will come when Castro feels the pressure enough and is pushed by the Soviets into negotiations — not necessarily with us — but with some of the Latin American countries for readmission to the Organization of American States, and a lifting of the severity of the embargoes and the boycotts. I think that's probable.

SEVAREID: You don't think it's for us to voluntarily lift this embargo?

LIPPMANN: No, we can afford to wait. He can't threaten us. He's no danger to us, as Senator Fulbright said, and we're in no hurry. He'll be the one who will have to be in a hurry.

SEVAREID: I think you once said — sometime ago — that if Castro were successful in what he's trying to do with Cuba, this would really be dangerous in the rest of Latin America.

LIPPMANN: Well, if he were able to produce a brilliant Communist state there in spite of us and in spite of everything, of course, it would be a very dangerous example. It's only as an example that you have to fear Castro. The agents and the certain amount of arms are really a trifling matter compared to the other. The example is what counts.

SEVAREID: Suppose other Latin American countries turn Communist in the meantime?

LIPPMANN: Well, things could go very badly, but we have to cross that bridge when we come to it, if we do.

SEVAREID: Mr. Lippmann, since you last talked into these cameras, this country has experienced a couple of historic things at least. One, the beginning of what some people call a Negro revolution, and then the abrupt ending of the Kennedy era. I wonder if you think enough time has gone by now so that one can judge John F. Kennedy and how history may judge him, say thirty years from now. How do you now feel about his time in the White House?

LIPPMANN: Well, I don't think enough time has gone by with the shock of his murder so close to us, and the people now are still either grieving deeply or missing something that fascinated them tremendously. But they are in no position to make a judgment or an appraisal.

SEVAREID: Well, what was it about him that so fascinated people?

LIPPMANN: His looks, and his way of dealing with

the thing, and the fact that he was a new kind of American politician. I'm not sure how much the country was at home with this new kind, but he was new and a whole new generation sort of pinned their hopes on his success.

SEVAREID: Was he successful in those three years?

LIPPMANN: That is something nobody can answer today. And that is the reason why any genuine historical judgment is quite impossible, because we have to see how a lot of the things that he is identified with come out. For example, he may have — and probably has — brought to an end the threat, for the foreseeable future, of nuclear war. But it's awfully early to be sure that that is true. Then, he initiated certain things at home, such as a new fiscal policy, a really serious attack on the problem of Negro rights — civil rights; and he was preparing — and President Johnson is carrying it on — the campaign against poverty. Until we know how those come out, we don't know what historians will say about him.

SEVAREID: Certainly his style, so called, was very different. How important do you think this matter of style is in a Chief Executive?

LIPPMANN: I think it's very important. That doesn't mean that there's only one style. I mean a man must be true to his own style, not to somebody else's style. And the Kennedy style was something that the country had never seen before in a President.

SEVAREID: What have been your impressions of President Johnson's method of conducting this office?

LIPPMANN: Well, my feeling about that is this: When President Kennedy was murdered, the situation abroad and at home was in a state of — I think you could fairly call it crisis. His own policies were blocked at home, and they were frustrated abroad, and the country was very deeply and bitterly divided about him. There was sectional feeling. There was class feeling. There was racial feeling. And Johnson — President Johnson, I should say — is by nature a healing man, a man who heals. And that's been his function — his mission — in his first hundred days, or four or five months, whatever it is.

SEVAREID: Are you saying, in effect, that while Johnson may not have the fervent phalanx of admirers in the country that Kennedy had, he has fewer enemies?

LIPPMANN: Oh, very many fewer. And the country is far more united and at peace with itself, except over the issue of Negro rights, than it has been for a long time.

SEVAREID: And you attribute that to the accession of a new President?

LIPPMANN: Well, I attribute it to the accession of this new President. Not any man who succeeded Kennedy could have done it. But this man's genius in politics, which he's tried out for years — ten, fifteen years in the Senate, and so on, and thirty years in Washington — has been finding the point at which a consensus — an agreement — is possible. He takes in a very broad area; and the country feels that about him, somehow, and he has responded to it.

SEVAREID: The President has done pretty well with the Congress. Perhaps better than Kennedy.

LIPPMANN: He's done extremely well. And he's done, I think, what President Kennedy could not have done had he lived.

SEVAREID: You felt last year, or a very few months ago rather, that the Congress was almost conducting a sit-down.

LIPPMANN: Oh, I spoke, I think, before of the crisis which existed when Kennedy was killed. The Senate had deliberately brought the Kennedy administration to a standstill, and they wouldn't even appropriate, perhaps, the appropriation bill. That's as near an absolute confrontation as you can get in our system of government. Now that's broken up, partly by the shock of the assassination, and partly by the skill of President Johnson.

SEVAREID: Well, every political leader has some flaws and faults. When you watch President Johnson at work, do you detect any particular weaknesses that may catch up with him?

LIPPMANN: Well, I suppose, yes. It comes out of his background and experience, and he is so much the product of the legislative branch of the government that his executive action is, and rightly most of the time, deeply attuned and extremely sensitive to what Congress wants. Now, you can't conduct foreign affairs wholly in that method. For example, I feel sure that the difficulty over Panama arose not over the words which were quarreled about but over the perhaps excessive fear that if a revised treaty is negotiated, as undoubtedly it will have to be sooner or later, it will be very difficult to pass it through the Senate. And I think President Johnson has done extremely well with this problem except now and then one sees, I think, an excessive deference to the prejudices — and what Senator Fulbright called the other day the myths — which exist in the Senate.

SEVAREID: Would it be a fair generalization at this point to say then that whether policies are wiser

or not, at least the machinery is better oiled and is
working better?

LIPPMANN: Well, the policies are the same.
There's no difference in policies between the two
Presidents. This should be known not as the Johnson administration, but as the Kennedy-Johnson administration. And it is a continuation. Every important measure and every important policy continues
from President Kennedy. And he would have to do
what Johnson is going to have to do before he gets
through — revise some of those policies. But they
started as Kennedy policies.

SEVAREID: So far this is more continuity than
transition, is it?

LIPPMANN: This is continuity.

SEVAREID: But at some point, President Johnson must have a Johnson stamp on all this, must he
not?

LIPPMANN: Well, not for the sake of his pride or
anything, but of course if he's re-elected and has a
substantial majority, not a hairline majority such as
Kennedy had, he will be able to do in a sense what
Eisenhower was in a position to do when he came in.
He was able to revise some of the old standards, old
stances, the old myths of his own party and of the
Congress and of the country. And that's going to be
Johnson's work, if he's re-elected.

SEVAREID: Are you one of those people who worry about the extreme pace of his personal activity, particularly in view of the fact that he has had one heart attack?

LIPPMANN: I'm going to leave that to his doctors and his wife. I don't think I'll answer that.

SEVAREID: Are you willing to make any prediction about who will be the Republican nominee?

LIPPMANN: Oh, I can't make a prediction. I think it lies between Nixon and Lodge, and conceivably Scranton. Well, the man I think has the greatest promise as a public man in the coming years is Scranton, but Scranton is not known. He's quite — really — badly — not experienced at all, and if I were his campaign manager, I'd run him for Vice President and get him well known, even though he was beaten.

SEVAREID: How do you account for this Lodge phenomenon? After all he's ten thousand miles away, saying nothing, and yet he's winning primaries.

LIPPMANN: Well, there are a number of reasons to explain it. First, "Nature abhors a vacuum." "Absence makes the heart grow fonder."

SEVAREID: Yes, but there's another old saying, "Out of sight, out of mind."

LIPPMANN: Yes, but he's not out of sight, you see, what with modern means of communication.

He's very visible, and then I think there's a genuine feeling that he is a moderate, he belongs to the wing of the party that has to be dominant if they're ever going to win. It's the Eisenhower wing of the party, really.

SEVAREID: Some romantic trappings in his present setting?

LIPPMANN: Romantic — he's out there doing a hard job, which people admire, public service at great considerable risk to his reputation and even to his self, physically, and all those things work in his favor as against the field.

SEVAREID: What works against him?

LIPPMANN: The politicians who worked with him in 1960 don't think he made a good campaign and don't like him. I think the straight machine politicians don't want to nominate him. That's his greatest difficulty.

SEVAREID: What about Mr. Nixon? Is he deeply entrenched in the affections of this party, or is he rather shopworn by now?

LIPPMANN: No, he's not entrenched in the affections of the party. His nomination would be the nomination of a caretaker for the party in a bad year. Nixon has — as a candidate — certain qualifications. He has a reputation for knowing a great

deal about foreign affairs and his party will talk
about foreign affairs a great deal. And he is an in-
fighter. They undoubtedly will have to try to do something to weaken President Johnson's personal stand-
ing in the country, and he's more willing to do it than
almost any candidate.

SEVAREID: You think that Goldwater and Rockefeller have pretty well run their course?

LIPPMANN: I think they've run their course.

SEVAREID: Well, what's the trouble then with
Governor Rockefeller? He's had a lot of Federal
Government experience — governor of the biggest state in the country. Why hasn't he done better
in this campaign?

LIPPMANN: Well, apart from the problems of his
private life and his marriage, he was the man best
suited by background and training to seize the middle ground for the Republicans, and he hasn't done
it. He's conducted a campaign in which he never
quite knows whether he's trying to be like Senator
Goldwater, or whether he's trying to be not like him.
And he's underestimated the American voter, which
I think is what the New Hampshire primary vote
shows. And that's probably the most dangerous thing
a politician can do. He's tried to get down to a level
which is below the level of the people who really

make opinion and decide elections, and they don't want to be talked down to. They know he's talking down. They know that Rockefeller isn't as folksy and palsy-walsy as he says he is, and this has been, I think, fatal to his campaign. He's done what a really good politician cannot do — he's stooped to conquer, and of course he's not conquering.

SEVAREID: Mr. Lippmann, I think about a year ago in one of these discussions, you said that perhaps the Republicans ought to nominate Mr. Goldwater and put to a test finally this idea that's persisted in the party since Taft's time, at least, that if you nominated what they call a real Republican, he could win. You'd bring a lot of voters out who don't come out normally. Have you changed your feeling about that?

LIPPMANN: Oh, yes. First of all, I wasn't really anxious to have Goldwater a candidate, but I thought as against John F. Kennedy it might have cleared the air very much. The real objection to it — nominating Goldwater — is that it would wreck the Republican party for maybe two elections.

SEVAREID: Why?

LIPPMANN: Because it would put the party in the control of a far-out extremist wing which never can win in this country. There aren't the votes there. New Hampshire was a good measure of that. There were — what did Senator Goldwater have — only clear less then twenty-five per cent of the vote. Well, I think that with the death of Kennedy, and with the very fragile character of Goldwater's support once he was exposed in front of television and in public meetings, that the unsuitability of his candidacy has become so evident that I don't think we need that test.

SEVAREID: Do you wish to speculate, Mr. Lippmann, about who you think might have the best chance on the Republican side?

LIPPMANN: I wouldn't say that any one of the candidates we hear about has a much better chance than any other one. The Republican problem is to rebuild their party, which is in very bad condition due to their division between the far right and the moderates.

SEVAREID: Is it a terribly important question just whom the Democrats nominate for Vice President?

LIPPMANN: My feeling is that President Johnson's position is unique in that he cannot be helped by anybody who is named as a possible candidate.

SEVAREID: Well, which of these various gentlemen mentioned for Vice President would be the greatest help to President Johnson?

LIPPMANN: That's not a good question, Eric, because I'm not that kind of a political dopester.

SEVAREID: Well, you said that nobody who is now named would be of great help. I don't quite understand you.

LIPPMANN: I mean that the President can win with any one of those people, and he won't win more because he has one of them on the ticket than if he didn't have them. Now, there are choices among them as to who would make the best President, and that is the real consideration in this case. That's the point I'm trying to make. That for him, the only real consideration is who would be a good successor.

SEVAREID: Well, since I'm not talking to the President of the United States now, but to Mr. Walter Lippmann, who do you think would be the best Vice Presidential candidate?

LIPPMANN: It lies between two men in my mind: Senator Humphrey and Secretary McNamara, and I think we'll have to wait a little longer to see how McNamara makes out in Vietnam, and how Humphrey makes out in civil rights before we need to come to any conclusion about it.

SEVAREID: Mr. McNamara as a Vice Presidential candidate presents an interesting problem. He's a Republican, isn't he?

LIPPMANN: Well, I suppose he was a Republican, but of course that's the way the Kennedy administration has been constructed — to put Republicans in key points. Because it's really — it was an attempt on Kennedy's part to create something like a coalition government.

SEVAREID: You don't think this party identification of McNamara's would present a real problem at a convention?

LIPPMANN: I think there'll be Republican politicians and Democratic politicians who may object, but I wouldn't think it would make any difference, if President Johnson decided that's the man he wanted.

SEVAREID: Mr. Lippmann, you haven't mentioned among possible Vice Presidential candidates the Attorney General, Robert Kennedy. Do you think he's going to play a part in this?

LIPPMANN: Well, he'll play a part, and he's a political power in the Democratic Party, but I don't see any reason why he should be nominated for Vice President.

SEVAREID: You make it sound as though President Johnson would be a very hard man to defeat next fall.

LIPPMANN: Well, I wouldn't like to have the job of trying to defeat him. Of course, if things go very sour, and we have an economic breakdown, or some catastrophe abroad, which nobody can foresee today, everything one says today might change. It's conceivable that something terrible will happen and that it would be easy for a Republican to win. But it isn't easy today, and I think all Republicans know that.

SEVAREID: If something were to happen that really made trouble for President Johnson, wouldn't it almost have to be something of a domestic nature? Foreign affairs, unless they're totally catastrophic, normally haven't affected incumbents so much, have they?

LIPPMANN: I agree with you. I mean as long as the country is united and trusts the President, he can suffer a great many setbacks abroad and not necessarily lose by it at all. After all, President Eisenhower accepted a good deal less than a victory in Korea.

SEVAREID: Yes, he did.

LIPPMANN: That was certainly a peace without victory if ever there was one. And the country liked it — really, they were glad it was over. It didn't hurt him politically.

SEVAREID: Do you think it might be possible that the civil rights demonstrations in the streets of this country this spring and summer might really get out of hand and provoke a reaction among white people to the extent that President Johnson could really be hurt next November?

LIPPMANN: Well, I think the whole civil rights affair — the bill and the situation which it springs from — are an explosive thing under our society, and that's one of the catastrophies — one of those things I said you couldn't estimate — when I said something terrible might happen. Yes, it's conceivable. It's conceivable that a long filibuster will produce race riots in which whites — in the North as well as the South — will join. Yes, it's possible.

SEVAREID: Do you think of the filibuster as a legitimate form of check and balance against the will of the majority?

LIPPMANN: I've always defended the filibuster or opposed an easy cloture — but not any cloture. I've always opposed it when the issue was one which would be far better dealt with if you could get the consent of the minority. I don't want to override the South, for example, by a fifty-one per cent majority. On the other hand, you get to a point, and I think — I'm sure we've reached it in the problem of civil rights and the Negro protest — where holding it up indefinitely is intolerable. You can't have filibusters in time of war. You can't have a filibuster which denies this country the right to promote the inter-

nal peace of this country, which is what the civil
rights bill is about. So I don't support this filibuster,
and I think after they've had a good, long talk about
it — it shouldn't be hurried — I'd like to see a cloture passed, if that is necessary, but I hope none will
be necessary because the value of the filibuster is
that in a crisis it could be a very great defense of
liberty in this country.

SEVAREID: Mr. Lippmann, there seems to be
nothing of a mighty and dramatic nature that the
United States can do abroad now. We have reached
a period of a great slowing down of these cataclysmic
events we've lived with. What is the task of this
country? A great country must have some great en-
terprise. What ought it to be? I presume it's here at
home, is it not?

LIPPMANN: Yes, it is. You see, we had to fight
World War Two. We had to fight the Cold War. We
had to conduct the race of armaments. We had to
nullify and neutralize — yes, nullify Soviet nuclear
power, and we've done that. We've succeeded. We're
out from under a terrible threat, but this doing all
that has been frightfully costly. It's cost not only
over half the Federal budget, but it's cost the time
and energy and emotional concern of our people for
twenty years. The result is we've had to neglect the
development of this vast country. And the result of

that neglect is seen in the condition of our schools, in the condition of our cities, in the backwardness of our transportation system, railroad transportation, and in a lot of other things. And now that the terrible danger is past — the critical danger — we can turn our attention to our own affairs without neglecting our responsibilities elsewhere.

VII

FEBRUARY 22, 1965

Lippmann and Eric Sevareid

In the months immediately preceding this broadcast former Vice President Lyndon B. Johnson had been elected President by an overwhelming majority and in his first messages to Congress had defined his goals for the Great Society. Nikita Khrushchev had been "retired" by the Politburo; Sir Winston Churchill, the greatest Englishman of this century, had died, and the Labour Party under Harold Wilson had come into power by a very narrow margin. There was no stable government in Vietnam, the leadership changing with dismaying frequency, as it had in France before de Gaulle; the retaliatory raids on Viet Cong installations by American-manned bombers had drawn sharp protests from Moscow and Peking, and in the American press petitions appeared asking for negotiation rather than escalation. In the Western Alliance there were such outspoken misgivings about the Multilateral Force that the project had been quietly put away in mothballs, and of the leaders General de Gaulle with his lone and lofty vision was regarded with a mixture of impatience and admiration.

February 22, 1965

SEVAREID: Mr. Lippmann, this is the twentieth year since the end of the great war. We seem to be surrounded by a lot of paradox. We're the most powerful country in the world, and we can't seem to find either victory or peace in a small Asiatic land. There's almost a feeling that this is a prewar period. What do you think the President's real choices are now in Vietnam?

LIPPMANN: The President has a very hard choice to make. He's really in a dilemma, and either horn of that dilemma is extremely uncomfortable, and unpleasant. One horn is to escalate, that is to widen and increase the war, which is a very terrible choice because it almost certainly would lead us into a war with China before it ended. And we can't tell what Russia would do in the case of a war with China. Anyway, the risks are incalculable of widening the war, and the President, of course, is doing his best to avoid that.

The other dilemma is to negotiate a truce in Vietnam. We're not sure that we can because the interior situation in South Vietnam is breaking up, crumbling, and that is what the victory of the Viet Cong is feeding upon. We're not sure that the Chinese or the North Vietnamese, who think they're winning — and have good reason to think that they're winning — would be willing to negotiate something that stopped them short of complete victory. Complete victory would be a collapse of the Vietnamese Government, and a setting up of a new government which would invite the United States to leave.

The reason that dilemma is so bad is not only that it would be embarrassing and humiliating, but because during the years we've been in there — whether we ought to have been there in the first place is another question — a great many Vietnamese have become dependent on us, and the chances for their future if we leave are very slim. I don't know that they'd all be liquidated, but some of them would have to flee the country, and we have a debt of honor to these Vietnamese who have thrown themselves on our side in this civil war. And therefore it's very hard for the President to choose that side which is disengagement. What he is doing now, of course, is to try to find something between these two extremes.

SEVAREID: Mr. Lippmann, you've called this a civil war. The administration talk is always about the intervention from North Vietnam, another state. You really think it is just a civil war?

LIPPMANN: I think it is, but like all civil wars, foreign outside powers intervene in them, and that's been true of every civil war you can think of, beginning with our own. The intervention from the outside is very important, but it isn't the revolution. The American Revolution wasn't made by the French, it was made by the Americans, and all these revolutions, the Russian Revolution, the Chinese Revolution, all were made by the people of the country itself, and that's true also in Vietnam, in my view.

SEVAREID: What is the most we can hope for as the outcome of negotiations, however it takes place?

LIPPMANN: The most we could hope for is that there will be a sufficient political truce in the civil war for a period of time — some years — so that they can adjust themselves to each other — I mean the people who have been fighting on opposite sides in the civil war. This can heal their wounds, and that's about all. I mean, we can't make South Vietnam, and we can't make Southeast Asia, an American outpost. We don't want to, the President says we don't want to. And we can't do it. What we can do is see that it doesn't become a Chinese military outpost, which is quite a different thing from saying that it will be eventually within the Chinese sphere of influence.

I don't know of any man living who thinks that thirty-five years from now, when the Chinese are one half of the whole human race, they aren't going to be the dominant power in Southeast Asia. Of course they are, but they're not there now, and we have to protect the people who would be liquidated, killed, really, persecuted if we suddenly disappeared. That's our problem.

SEVAREID: Isn't much of the dilemma whether we actually can get the negotiations going?

LIPPMANN: It is a real question whether we can rally enough world opinion, and enough diplomatic support from the Soviet Union particularly, and from Japan, and India and other Asiatic countries, something to induce them to negotiate. So we have to find ways of going behind the scenes. And there are many ways behind the scenes to China, to Moscow, to Tokyo and New Delhi, and so on, also to London and Paris, ways to create a situation diplomatically which nobody in the world can define today, but which will make it advantageous and necessary for the Communists to negotiate.

SEVAREID: You'd need a cease-fire from the Viet Cong before such negotiations.

LIPPMANN: You'd have to do the diplomatic exploration which I've been talking about, which is not a conference, you'll have to do that before there's a

cease-fire. Now, one of the terms I would think indispensable to a negotiation, or any kind of talk, back
and forth, would be that we would not withdraw
while the thing was going on. You see, we are faced
with an ultimatum — have been from Hanoi, and
Peking — that we must get out, and then talk. Now,
that we can't do, because that means abandoning
all our friends and all our interests and that would
be scuttling the ship.

SEVAREID: Mr. Lippmann, there are complaints
in the press that this is not only an undeclared war
we're conducting, but an unexplained war, and the
President is criticized for not talking to the public
about this involvement. Do you think he should?

LIPPMANN: Well, I think he's in a very difficult
position. An irresponsible journalist can tell the
truth, but if the President of the United States tells
it, morale will probably collapse in Saigon. That government would just blow up. If he tells what he
wants to do, on what terms he would be willing to
consider negotiating, they'll immediately reject them
publicly, which makes it impossible for them to accept it in the end, and here there'll be a great out-
cry from the war hawks that he's appeasing. So he's
caught in a jam and I don't think he can explain the
war more — I think he has to work, because of
the nature of this involvement, and that's one of the

mischiefs of getting involved in it — he has to work through really what amounts to secret diplomacy.

SEVAREID: In your own work here in Washington, do you really find a serious war party, war hawks so to speak, who want to make a big roar out of this war in Vietnam?

LIPPMANN: They're very strong and powerful. I don't think they're a big camp, but I think they're quite powerful and influential.

SEVAREID: Do you care to say in what areas they would be found?

LIPPMANN: Well, I think as a matter of fact, they would be found in the military area, and to some degree in the diplomatic area. But they're not found in the interior and at the top of the White House. That I feel sure of.

SEVAREID: Well, in the White House there's only one top man, so I assume that you mean that you're convinced that the President —

LIPPMANN: I mean the President is not a war hawk. The war hawks want to bomb Hanoi, and all the industries. They want to knock out the whole industrial system of North Vietnam, and if anybody says well, the Chinese will come in, intervene, the war hawk says then bomb China too. The President's policy in bombing is a very strictly controlled and regulated policy. We're not bombing North Vietnam, we're bombing the borderland above the Seventeenth Parallel, which is a rather empty country, and we signal our attacks and they know when we're coming. There's no surprise attack, and they are really public relations jobs, much more than they are military jobs.

SEVAREID: They're political bombing —

LIPPMANN: They're political bombings, and they don't kill many people. I don't think they kill anybody.* There's no evidence that they do, because what we bomb is wooden sheds. Now, I don't think there's any doubt at all that if we bomb North Vietnam the way the war hawks want it bombed, and make it uninhabitable, the Vietnamese Army, which by the way is the largest land army in eastern Asia except China's, will move right down into South Vietnam where they can't be bombed, and where there are rich prizes, and I don't think South Vietnam will resist them. They couldn't.

Now, the war hawk's answer to that is: Yes, it's so important we must send troops in. And they're talking — when you really press them — in hundreds of thousands of American troops to hold the line. If we are in the position in Vietnam that England was un-

* This was spoken on February 22, 1965.

der with Churchill in 1940, if they were on our beaches, we'd have to do that, but eight thousand miles away, I don't think we have to do that, and I hope we won't!

SEVAREID: Suppose, Mr. Lippmann, that in the showdown the war hawks have their way. Then what happens?

LIPPMANN: At first, if the war hawks prevail, and we become involved in a big war, they will rejoice, but in the end the people will weep.

SEVAREID: You don't agree, then, with those who say that South Vietnam is another Berlin or Korea?

LIPPMANN: No. It's not a Korea because it's not an invasion, as Korea was. That was an open, old-fashioned invasion by an army that crossed a frontier and you had battles in the open. This is not. This is like a flood, like water spreading, and you can't beat it back or shoot it with a shotgun. It won't go back.

SEVAREID: One would suppose the war hawks learned their own lesson, a military lesson from Korea when the Chinese came into it.

LIPPMANN: Well, they will tell you, they say the Korean syndrome, they call it, has made the Americans frightened. Well, I don't know, maybe they've learned from experience. That's another way of putting it.

SEVAREID: Mr. Lippmann, there are many people here who think that if we do withdraw from that part of Southeast Asia, however it happens, that we will have suffered an enormous and historic American defeat.

LIPPMANN: Well, I tell you, if we made a mistake — and I think we made a mistake to involve ourselves in a war on the land in Asia — contrary to all previous American teaching, military teaching and doctrine, we have to expect to pay some price for it. We can't expect to get out gloriously from a mistake. But if you mean that the United States will cease to be a power in Asia if it negotiates itself out of Vietnam eventually, that answer is not true. The United States controls the whole Pacific Ocean, all the water, all the air above it, and all the air over the way into the interior of China and so on. Now that is a situation which has never existed before in American history, and that will continue to exist.

SEVAREID: I take it you're not concerned about any immediate toppling of dominoes in the rest of Southeast Asia.

LIPPMANN: Not immediate. But I never deceive myself. I never believed in going into Southeast Asia, I've said many times, and written it in all kinds of things. I've never believed we ought to be there, but as long as we are there, I believe what we have to do is to stay there long enough to make the process orderly rather than disorderly and violent.

SEVAREID: Does this government have an overall policy for Asia?

LIPPMANN: We have objective commitments which are not necessarily policy for the long run. I'm not talking about tomorrow, but the far future, ten, fifteen, twenty years from now. We have these commitments as a result of our victory over the Japanese Empire in the Second World War. We find ourselves in places where we can't expect to stay for the rest of time. We aren't going to stay forever in South Korea, and we aren't going to stay forever in South Vietnam, nor forever in Taiwan, nor in Okinawa, which is part of Japan. If we have any sense, any maturity, we will adjust our minds to the fact that over the generations the tide is going to recede to something more normal and natural.

SEVAREID: What you're saying, then, as I understand it, is that in the long run we must be prepared to live with Chinese Communist domination of Southeast Asia.

LIPPMANN: The situation for us in the Pacific is very like what happened in Europe with the Russians. We have lived with the Soviet domination of

Eastern Europe since 1945, and look at it now. It's dissolving. If we can hold China, in a great military sense, from building a navy like the Japanese Navy was at Pearl Harbor, from becoming a real threat to our peace, and wait as we've waited with the Soviet Union, in the end the same forces will work in China that have worked in the Soviet Union. She'll relax her grip.

SEVAREID: But East Europe is confronted with a countervailing force in the sense of the great weight and prosperity of West Germany and the rest of West Europe pressing close on East Europe's very borders. You wouldn't have that, really, would you, in the Far East? Where would the contrast and the other force come from?

LIPPMANN: The best I would expect on looking at the long run is if we can get that kind of pause, and interlude — that, I think, is the best we can hope for. For instance, I think that Vietnam, which was always anti-Chinese, will follow the same line that Tito has followed in Europe as against the Soviet Union. It will be Socialist or Communist in a manner of speaking, because those words don't apply very well in Asia, but it'll be tending to be anti-Chinese and independent and that will be, from our point of view, quite satisfactory.

SEVAREID: Do you fear the Chinese possession of the bomb?

LIPPMANN: I certainly do. I fear it very much. I'm not having hysterics about it, because it's a long way off. And I'd be willing, I haven't absolutely made up my mind about it, but I think we probably could afford to offer the countries that are threatened by the bomb, which would be India, Japan — those would be the two important countries; they can't use the bomb on South Vietnam, or something like that — India and Japan, a guarantee not that we'd defend them with troops and ships and everything else, airplanes, but that if they are hit with a nuclear bomb, we'll hit back with a nuclear bomb. We could give a nuclear guarantee to them, and while I'm not sure that that's the right policy, I think we ought to consider it very carefully.

SEVAREID: Well then, that would make a full circle, wouldn't it, of American commitment? We have made this commitment for Europe, for Latin America under Mr. Kennedy, at the time of the Cuban missile crisis, and now you would include Asia too.

LIPPMANN: That is a commitment which we are able to fulfill. Holding villages in the jungles of Vietnam is not a commitment that the American troops can really fulfill.

SEVAREID: Mr. Lippmann, do you think what's happened recently in Vietnam, including our bombing, has altered the relations between Moscow and Peking?

LIPPMANN: Moscow is forced to align itself with Peking, but the underlying differences between those two powers are so deep that I don't think in the long run they can become one power again, and I think therefore we can count on, in this diplomatic offensive which I was talking about before, on quiet Russian support. First of all they have a territorial conflict, over a frontier which is the longest in the world, and the most badly defined, stretches 4000 miles across Asia between Siberia, Soviet Siberia, and China, with territory in dispute all along the way. That doesn't make for peace, and there's been a lot of fighting going on that never got reported on that frontier.

The other thing is that they're in different stages of development. The Russians have passed the revolutionary stage in their own development. They have a going society with big industry, and they don't have to keep the country in a state of war alarm — war tension — in order to get the people to endure the hardships that the regime requires. China doesn't want a war any more than Russia does, but she wants a state of war feeling, because she needs it for her own affairs, and Russia needs the opposite. She needs intercourse and commerce with the West. That's the original root of the quarrel between Khrushchev and Mao Tse-tung, and it continues with Khrushchev's successors, and it is an irreconcilable difference.

SEVAREID: Well, when China is a highly industrialized country, she's apt to be much more cautious, is she not? She'll be more vulnerable to atomic attack and destruction, for one thing, than she is as a village.

LIPPMANN: She'll go through the same evolution that every revolutionary society goes through. She'll become middle class, which is what the Russians are becoming. And when they're middle class, they don't like to have their property destroyed, and their families broken up, and their savings lost, and in other words, they become soft. And that softening process has happened in Russia, and it will happen if we can hold off war long enough, for say fifteen or twenty years, in China.

SEVAREID: Mr. Lippmann, may I turn to our relations with Europe now for a moment. There's a sense here, in Washington, that President Johnson has changed the terms of reference in our relations with the NATO Alliance countries; what is this change?

LIPPMANN: He has changed them, I think, and changed them for the better. After the World War, and up to President Johnson's time, the United States was not only the protector of Europe, the defender and military protector, but it was the banker, and it was the general political and moral boss, superintendent at least, of Europe. And in the course of that, we got ourselves very badly entangled, first with the British, who thought they were our special friend — which resulted in their being excluded from the Common Market by General de Gaulle. Then we got into a tangle with the Germans, who thought they were the special favorites of the United States. In those days, Chancellor Adenauer was the Chancellor of Germany. He was our chief adviser on European affairs.

We ought not to have special favorites among our allies, and President Johnson, who has kept on excellent terms with the British, and with the Germans, has ended that. The key to that whole business came out in the proposal to create a multilateral mixed-manned nuclear fleet, which the Germans would have owned forty per cent of, and that aroused fury all over — in France, among all the people who fear Germany — and there are a great many people who still fear Germany in Europe — all over Eastern Europe, and in the Soviet Union, and he just put that away, he suspended it.

SEVAREID: Is this what you once called "masterly inactivity?"

LIPPMANN: Masterly inactivity. You see, when you are no longer needed as the leader of Europe, then the right thing to do is to stop trying to lead it. Let Europe develop in its own way, which is I think going quite satisfactorily.

SEVAREID: Is it going in the direction of a more cohesive united Europe?

LIPPMANN: Yes, it's going in the direction of the breaking down of the Iron Curtain, between the two halves of Europe. This is a process of trade, and sport, and cultural communication between the two halves of Europe.

SEVAREID: Do you think we could have arrived at that rather favorable point had we not taken the great leadership for many years, had we not had all these troops in Europe?

LIPPMANN: We had to do it. It was under our protection, and with our financial help, that Europe recovered, but it has recovered. It's like a family, you have to recognize that the child has grown up, it has grown up and you can't treat it as if it were a baby.

SEVAREID: Mr. Lippmann, in Germany now there seems to be a revival of interest in the reunification of that country. Do you see this coming about?

LIPPMANN: I think it's going to come. I'm not surprised at the revival of interest, because Germany, divided as it is, not even in possession of its own capital, is a sick country. It's done very well economically, but politically it's sick. And it will never be well until it's reunified. The reunification can come about, I think, only by the process I was talking about, by the gradual weaving together of the two parts of Europe. When that has taken place, Germany will be reunited in the process.

SEVAREID: President de Gaulle is now the last of the great wartime leaders of the West, and the most powerful political personality in Europe. Why don't we get along with him better? Who misunderstands whom?

LIPPMANN: Well, there's a good deal of misunderstanding both ways, I don't doubt. Memories of the war. He and President Roosevelt didn't get on. He and Churchill had difficulties, but they got on better than President Roosevelt and de Gaulle. But the basic difficulty about de Gaulle, I find this from lots of people, de Gaulle is like a man who can't see very clearly what's right in front of him, who sees pretty well what's across the room, or halfway down the street, but who sees absolutely perfectly what's in the distance. He has the farthest vision, he can see further, than any man in our time, and I don't even exclude Churchill. De Gaulle foresaw, at the worst moment in the fall of France, how in the end the war would be won, namely by the coming in of Russia and the United States. That kind of vision is very annoying to public men who don't see that far.

On the other hand, the fact that he doesn't see very clearly in front of him, and stumbles over the furniture, is very annoying too, and he kicks their shins as he goes, that sort of thing. But that's the problem, and the genius of his vision is so important. For instance, he has foreseen, and we have followed — we didn't take it from him, but we are following the same policy by the same logic — he has foreseen that the reunification of Germany and of Europe would have to come about through increasing connections with Eastern Europe, between East and West Europe. He's doing that. He's been much closer to the East Europeans than anybody. Well, we're doing that too. In the Far East, it is very annoying to us that he recognized China. It was a sign of very great vision, to see that there'd never be peace in the Far East until it was made with China. You can't make it with anybody else, and that kind of evasion is the cause of difficulty.

SEVAREID: You think President Johnson ought to meet personally with President de Gaulle any time soon?

LIPPMANN: I'm in no hurry for that. I don't think they're built to understand each other too well. I think they'd better meet through very skillful ambassadors.

SEVAREID: Apparently the President wants to go to Europe some time soon, and to Russia too. Do you think the time is really ripe for that?

LIPPMANN: Well, if he asked my advice, which he hasn't, I would not advise him to go.

SEVAREID: Why not?

LIPPMANN: I'd advise him to get the Great Society going in this country, and we'd have something in the bank to talk about. His style isn't the style that Europeans naturally understand, this old-fashioned American style, and I wouldn't think he'd do too well, and I don't think you can accomplish anything by face-to-face talk with a man like de Gaulle, or with a man like Kosygin.

SEVAREID: It's just a mass public relations exercise.

LIPPMANN: It will be public relations, and too many reporters, and too many cameras, and too many everything, and it wouldn't work, and they'd all say things that they'd wish they hadn't said, when it's over. So I'm in favor of the President staying home. If he wants to travel I think he might go to South America, one or two trips. That might be useful.

SEVAREID: Mr. Lippmann, if the President does go to Russia, he'll find a new regime now, Mr. Khrushchev has gone since we last had these conversations. Why do you think he disappeared, and what's different about this new regime?

LIPPMANN: Well, I don't know. I haven't been to Russia. I don't think — the cards are not face up on the table. We can't read it clearly. If you look at the underlying forces, Kosygin has just as great an interest as Khrushchev had, first of all in avoiding nuclear war with the United States, and also an interest in getting better relations with Eastern Europe and the Western world for economic reasons.

I've been told by a relative of one of the new rulers of Russia, who was here on a scholarship, that they got tired of Khrushchev's inefficiency, and his wildness. He promised things that he hadn't the authority to promise. And that was the reason they said let's get this more organized, and more orderly, and the very noticeable fact is that first they've divided Khrushchev's jobs into two jobs. Khrushchev was both Secretary of the Communist Party, which was considered the most powerful job, and the other job, he was Prime Minister of the Soviet Union, or Chairman or whatever they call it. Now they have two men, Kosygin and Brezhnev, and it's very interesting, they no longer travel together. They don't go to foreign countries together as in the early days before Khrushchev got the both jobs, he used to travel around with his other man.

SEVAREID: Bulganin.

LIPPMANN: Bulganin.

SEVAREID: Well, I suppose one of these two men must be the prevailing one eventually.

LIPPMANN: Unless there's been a change and — Russia is evolving — unless the evolution means that the Communist Party is no longer the militant world party that it was when Khrushchev first came into power.

SEVAREID: The established church instead of church militant, in other words.

LIPPMANN: Yes.

SEVAREID: Mr. Lippmann, about Great Britain, I think you were there recently. There seems to be a feeling of deep crisis about that country. Financial crisis for one thing, a government with a bare majority in Parliament. What is really happening with them?

LIPPMANN: There is a deep crisis in Great Britain, and it may be that the historians will say that it was Labour Party's misfortune to come into power too soon, because the things that prevent the Labour Party from doing what it says it wants to do, and may be able to do, which is to revivify Great Britain from within, its industrial life and its technology and its education, have to be postponed because they're still dealing with the remnants of their empire out in Malaya, all the way from Aden to Singapore, and with the remnants of their old sterling area, which is a remnant from the days when London was the banker of the world. Now Labour is having the job of dealing with that, and that's a job that should be done by Conservatives. That's their business.

SEVAREID: Mr. Lippmann, did you follow the Churchill funeral ceremonies on television?

LIPPMANN: I did.

SEVAREID: Well, what was the real significance in your mind of the enormous emotional impact of this? Merely the man as a personality, a great turning point in British history? What was it?

LIPPMANN: Oh, I think the fundamental emotion here, at least the one I felt, and I assume that other people felt — was one of immense gratitude to this man who had saved the world from Nazism and

Fascism. That's one of the great achievements of a single man in modern history.

SEVAREID: You mean, he did this?

LIPPMANN: He did. Without him, there was no reason to think that Great Britain could have resisted, or would have resisted.

SEVAREID: Did the funeral of this man, then, represent in a sense the burial of the British Lion that the world has known for three hundred years?

LIPPMANN: Well, I've heard people say that, but I don't think we're in a position to reach any such conclusion. I don't think so. I remember a song of Beatrice Lillie's, "There's Life in the Old Girl Yet," and we'll probably see that.

SEVAREID: Were you particularly upset about the fact that the Vice President did not go to the funeral?

LIPPMANN: No, I think the President made a mistake about this, when he couldn't go himself. I think he was too sick. His head wasn't clear enough to have done the obvious and right thing to do, which was to appoint General Eisenhower as his personal representative. Eisenhower was already invited by Lady Churchill to come to the funeral, but he should have been the American representative. He was the man who was Supreme Commander under Churchill, he had been President twice, he was the man. There was too much confusion in the White House to think out the right thing. I don't blame the President for not wanting the Vice President to leave when he himself was sick.

SEVAREID: Mr. Lippmann, a moment ago you said that the President, before he goes abroad, ought to get the Great Society program really working. How do you define this program, the Great Society? What's the essence of it?

LIPPMANN: Well, I think the best way to answer that is to say how it differs from the New Deal, the Fair Deal or the Square Deal, or all those deals that have preceded it. All of those older deals were based on the assumption that the amount of wealth in the country was more or less fixed, and that in order to help the poor, or to educate people or to do anything, you had to divide the wealth, take away from the well-to-do and give it either to the government or to the poor or somebody. That's why it's called a New Deal. It's the same pack, but you deal it differently — or a Square Deal, and so on.

Now, the Great Society is a result of a revolution that's occurred, a silent and beneficent revolution that's occurred in our generation, under which, we have learned, not perfectly because it's very difficult — it's a new art — we have learned how to control, regulate, and promote the production of wealth in an advanced industrial society. We are able to produce more wealth by putting on taxes, interest rates, and all the budgetary arrangements that we use, and make the thing grow, and we finance the new developments, education and everything that we talk about in the Great Society, the beautifying of cities, and everything of that sort out of the taxes on the increase of wealth that we're able to produce. We increased the wealth, the product of the United States by, I don't know, thirty billions last year. The taxes on that will pay for the whole of the Great Society, and nobody is any poorer, everybody's richer. Now, that is what the Great Society — that's its basis.

SEVAREID: Well, what's the single most important aspect of the President's program?

LIPPMANN: It's education, because it's like a vestibule from which all the corridors lead out. Unless you have education you cannot take away from the poorest part of the population the thing which keeps them poor, their inability to earn — they haven't learned enough and been trained enough to keep a good job, to do a good job. It also leads to research, to production of people to increase the scientific knowledge and the technical knowledge. It's the basis of making the democracy work.

SEVAREID: Mr. Lippmann, do you agree with the claims of some people in the press that President Johnson in trying to govern by consensus, so to speak, is refusing to spend any of his political capital; that he doesn't want to lose any of his mass public support; that a great President ought to be more courageous on that score. Do you feel that way?

LIPPMANN: On the contrary, I am in entire sympathy with him. It applies internally. Now, when you get abroad, that's another question. But within the country, the only real way to solve a problem like, for instance, the racial problem, is by having an overwhelming majority in favor of enforcement of civil rights. A consensus really means that about between sixty-five and seventy-five per cent of the people are in favor of the policy, that's really what it means. Not everybody's going to be in favor of it, and that's what the President had — he was in that range, when he was elected — and that's what he's trying to conserve. And he's quite right to conserve it. He will, if anybody can, solve the civil rights problem in the United States; it will be done that way, having the law, enforcing the law, but getting observance of the law by consent, voluntary consent, by a great mass of people.

The same is true of capital and labor. You can't solve their problems, except by a consensus, and the same is true of that argument we have heard so much about, the welfare state, and what do you do for the poor, and what do you do for the rich and all that. Now, consensus politics is possible only in a society which has reached the kind of revolutionary condition that we have, where we can control the output of wealth.

SEVAREID: Mr. Lippmann, most of us don't think of President Johnson as a philosopher in any formalized sense, or an ideologist in any sense. What's the secret of his appeal to the people?

LIPPMANN: The root of it is that he is really one of them, to a degree which very few Presidents in recent times have been. He doesn't have to be told what simple Americans, farmers, businessmen, are thinking. He already feels it himself. It's in him, and they know he feels it, and that's what gives — that's what creates the relationship between them.

SEVAREID: Well, does he have that quality of appreciation instinctively, more than President Kennedy, or President Eisenhower?

LIPPMANN: He does indeed. If you think of their careers, as compared with his, you'll see that they were as compared with Johnson, outsiders, coming into the political life of this country. But he's right in the heart of it, where it grows, and the thing is in him. He doesn't have to be taught it.

SEVAREID: Mr. Lippmann, since we last had one of these conversations, we had quite a considerable national election. The Republican Party, in terms of offices held at all levels in the country, is at its lowest point in about thirty years. Are we in danger of a one-party system here?

LIPPMANN: No, we're in no danger of having a one-party system. We may have a condition which we've had several times before in our history, when one party was predominant for a generation. But the party system always revives in a free country and we're a free country, so there's no danger. What is needed is for the other party to mean something and correct its mistakes. The great mistake of the Republican Party since the time of Theodore Roosevelt is that it quarreled with the intellectual community in the United States, and alienated them, and then under McCarthy's regime persecuted them, and they all went over to the Democrats and that gave the Democrats an intellectual capacity for dealing with issues that the Republicans simply didn't have.

SEVAREID: Is that a more serious alienation than the alienation of the Negroes in recent times, or labor?

LIPPMANN: The alienation of the Negroes is a very serious thing, and it probably cannot be corrected by this generation of Republican leaders. I mean by the leaders like Dirksen and Nixon. They participated in this process, they connived at it, and they will not be able to recover. But the younger people who are not burned in that fire, they may be able to do it. The obvious example is Congressman Lindsay in New York. Congressman Taft in Ohio, who was just beaten because of the Johnson landslide, who would otherwise be elected. Men now around forty. They never will reconstitute the party with the old war-horses who ran it into the ditch this time.

SEVAREID: Mr. Lippmann, this is the twentieth year since the birth of the United Nations. President Kennedy, I think, once called it the keystone of our foreign policy. Most people in the world seem to have great hopes for it. What do you think now about its present condition, and its prospects?

LIPPMANN: Well, I think it's in great difficulties. It's going through a crisis. The League of Nations and the United Nations, these two versions of the same idea, both required before they could operate successfully, that peace should be made. The reason the League of Nations failed was that it couldn't make a peace, it needed to have a peace to keep. The same is happening to the United Nations. It's in such grave difficulty because there's been no peace in Europe since the Second World War — Berlin, you know, the occupation, the continuing division — and there's no peace in Asia, and I don't expect that the United Nations can make that peace. The great powers have got to make the peace.

After it's made, and on the basis of its being made, the United Nations can function to keep it from tipping over; keeping order and balance — that is the crucial question not merely for the United Nations but for the world, whether we can bridge the next ten or fifteen years without war, in which case the United Nations will survive, and so will the peace of the world.

SEVAREID: But surely in this revolutionary time, there will always be outbreaks of one kind or another in many, many places.

LIPPMANN: There'll be outbreaks and, of course, the world is in ferment, and moving very rapidly, but the great power confrontations, which are a very different thing from rioting in the Congo, or a place like that, those great power confrontations have to be put in order, in some balance that is acceptable to the great powers.

SEVAREID: Would any institutional reorganization of the United Nations be of much value?

LIPPMANN: Well, I think we made a great mistake about the United Nations in 1949. We had wanted to use the United Nations to prevent wars and troubles breaking out, and the Soviet Union vetoed everything, and we wanted to get around the veto, and so we decided to give the power to keep the peace to the General Assembly, where we then had a perfectly clear and certain majority. Now, that is the decision which the Soviet Union is rebelling against. That's why they won't pay their dues, because they won't admit that the General Assembly ever had the right to raise an army and use it for peace-keeping purposes, and today we admit in theory that actually, we don't want to have the General Assembly commit us to go into war anywhere. We're not really arguing with the Russians. We're just saying these were the rules: The UN is bankrupt, Congress won't appropriate money if you don't pay up, if we have to pay all the bills, so pay up and then we'll go on from there. That's the situation as I understand it.

SEVAREID: Would there be any great advantage in putting the decisive power back in the Security Council?

LIPPMANN: The advantage of it is that that's the only place you can put decisive power. When you have decisive power, you have to give a veto. The Senate of the United States would never have ratified the Charter if we hadn't had a veto. And if the Senate of the United States were asked today, would you be willing to go to war if 75 of the 112 nations in the General Assembly voted you to go, but you didn't want to go, would you go? Well, of course you wouldn't go.

SEVAREID: The whole affair in the Congo beginning in 1960, when the UN tried to intervene and stabilize it, has damaged the UN in more than financial ways certainly. Now what about Africa and this central part of it, the Congo? How far ought we to go in trying to stabilize that place?

LIPPMANN: Well, we've always known, we knew back in 1960, when the Congo was liberated, or made independent, we knew then that we didn't want to get in there. We were afraid that the Russians would come in and therefore we turned to the United Nations and asked Dag Hammarskjold to take care of the Congo, keep it in order so that we wouldn't get involved and the Russians wouldn't get involved. And that's how the United Nations got in there, and that was done successfully for quite a long time. The original idea of giving it to the United Nations was correct. The United States has no business becoming militarily involved in Africa. It's bad enough to be involved in Southeast Asia, but to be involved in Africa too would be the height of absurdity, and we couldn't do everything at once.

SEVAREID: You're not terribly concerned about what happens in the middle of Africa, are you?

LIPPMANN: I'm rather concerned, but I don't take the thing ideologically as seriously as some people do. I think the war and trouble in the eastern Congo with the Chinese mixing in and so on is tribal fighting and not really a question of Communism or anti-Communism, and even if it were, what difference does it make in that corner of the middle of Africa, and if it does make a difference, what can we do about it, and why should we have to do it?

SEVAREID: Well, Mr. Lippmann, there is a great argument which gets more critical every year about just how far we ought to go in many places in the world in terms of our involvement, even our economic involvement. Now, why all this disenchantment about American economic and diplomatic interventions around the world?

LIPPMANN: I think basically it's come about because we have involved ourselves in too many places and we couldn't fulfill the promises we made when we went in, and therefore the intervention reacted against us. So our involvement causes not friendliness to the United States but unfriendliness, and we have to concentrate and focus our effort.

SEVAREID: One manifestation has been this great

rave of riots and burnings of our information offices, libraries, attacking embassies. How far can a great power tolerate this, really? Do we just continue to stand by and just ask for apologies?

LIPPMANN: Well, I think what we ought to do in a place like say Cairo, if they burned down our library, is leave it burned down. Just leave it there. Don't rebuild it, let it stand there as a monument to the thing. I think they'll soon want to clean it up themselves.

SEVAREID: You mentioned Cairo, and President Nasser. Sukarno of Indonesia is another example. It would appear that foreign aid from this country is becoming a political instrument in the hands of the recipients rather than the donor.

LIPPMANN: Well, I think I'm right in saying that Sukarno told us to go jump in the lake or something like that about our aid, and I would just stop it.

SEVAREID: Nasser also said we could take our aid and jump in the lake.

LIPPMANN: I'd stop the aid.

SEVAREID: You would?

LIPPMANN: I'd send him a formal note and say, you are reported as saying you don't want our aid. Don't you want our aid? And let him say which he wants.

SEVAREID: Then why don't we stop it?

LIPPMANN: Well don't ask me why we don't stop it. I think I would stop it if I had anything to say about it.

SEVAREID: Mr. Lippmann, the brunt of much of what you said in this hour is to the effect that we are overextended in the world, we are in too many places, we will have to pull in our horns to a considerable extent. Is it fair to say that Walter Lippmann, 1965, has become an isolationist?

LIPPMANN: Well, I don't think those words mean anything, or at least I don't care whether anybody uses them. I don't care about the word isolationism, and I don't care about the word appeasement. I'm interested in the rights and needs and responsibilities of the United States. We are not the policeman of mankind. We are not able to run the world, and we shouldn't pretend that we can. Let us tend to our own business, which is great enough as it is. It's very great. We have neglected our own affairs. Our education is inadequate, our cities are badly built, our social arrangements are unsatisfactory. We can't wait another generation. Unless we can surmount this crisis, and work and get going onto the path of a settlement in Asia, and a settlement in Europe, all of these plans of the Great Society here at home, all the plans for the rebuilding of backward countries in other continents will all be put on the shelf, because war interrupts everything like that.

SEVAREID: Mr. Lippmann, thank you very much.

Index

53; does not recognize East Germany, 79; Berlin negotiations, 72-78, 102-108; special relationship with France, 133; center government in, 135; relations with East Europe, 166; and Multilateral Fleet, 211

Willkie, Wendell, political ideology, 154

Wilson, Harold, 124, 196

Wilson, Woodrow, 17

World War I: Presidential leadership after, 14; postwar Europe, 131

World War II: Japanese surrender, 21; turning point, 99; postwar Europe, 130-131, 174; postwar world situation, 174